THROUGH A WOMAN'S EYE

PIONEERING PHOTOGRAPHERS IN RURAL UPSTATE

BY DIANE GALUSHA

WITH KAREN MARSHALL

FOR THE

DELAWARE COUNTY HISTORICAL ASSOCIATION

BLACK DOME PRESS CORP.

RR1 BOX 422, HENSONVILLE, NY 12439

(518) 734-6357 FAX (518) 734-5802

First Edition, 1994

Published by Black Dome Press Corp.

RR1, Box 422

Hensonville, NY 12439

(518)734-6357

Fax (518) 734-5802

Library of Congress Catalog Card Number: 93-74182

ISBN 1-883789-00-1

Cover Design by Artemisia, Inc., Windham, NY 12496

Printed in the USA

ACKNOWLEDGEMENTS

EVERY BOOK MAKES A UNIQUE JOURNEY TO PUBLICATION. AND AS IS OFTEN THE CASE, SERENDIPITY PLAYS A ROLE. THIS BOOK FIRST BECAME A POSSIBILITY WHEN WRITER CAROLYN BENNETT BECAME ENCHANTED WITH ANNA CARROLL'S PHOTOGRAPHS AT A LOCAL GALLERY EXHIBIT. SHE IMMEDIATELY CONTACTED DEBORAH ALLEN, PUBLISHER OF BLACK DOME PRESS, AND THEY BOTH DECIDED THERE WAS A BOOK IN THE MAKING. AND NOT JUST ANY BOOK. AS ANY STUDENT OF NEW YORK STATE HISTORY KNOWS, THE ROLE WOMEN HAVE PLAYED IN ITS CULTURAL PAST IS LARGELY UNDOCUMENTED. THIS WAS AN OPPORTUNITY TO PUT INTO PRINT A WORK THAT WOULD IN SOME SMALL MEASURE REDEEM THAT CONTRIBUTION.

ALLEN, IN TURN, APPROACHED LINDA NORRIS, DIRECTOR OF THE DELAWARE COUNTY HISTORICAL ASSOCIATION (DCHA), WHO WAS SIMILARLY INTRIGUED. SHE SUGGESTED EXPANDING THE SCOPE OF THE BOOK TO INCLUDE THE WORK OF TWO OTHER PIONEERING PHOTOGRAPHERS, LENA UNDERWOOD AND EDNA BENEDICT. FROM THAT MOMENT ON, LINDA NORRIS BECAME THE GUIDING SPIRIT BEHIND THE BOOK, CONTRIBUTING HER KNOWLEDGE AND ORGANIZATIONAL SKILLS, MOBILIZING TALENT AND RESOURCES EACH STEP OF THE WAY.

WITH THE COOPERATION OF THE COOPERSTOWN GRADUATE PROGRAM, KAREN MARSHALL WAS SELECTED TO RESEARCH THESE WOMEN'S LIVES FOR HER MASTER'S THESIS. UPON COMPLETION OF MARSHALL'S THOROUGH INVESTIGATIVE WORK, DIANE GALUSHA, WELL-KNOWN LOCAL HISTORIAN AND NEWSPAPER EDITOR, WAS BROUGHT ON BOARD TO WRITE THE BOOK.

DREW HARTY AND JOHN JACKSON WORKED TO CREATE PUBLICATION-QUALITY PRINTS FROM THE HISTORIC NEGATIVES. TALENTED PHOTOGRAPHERS THEMSELVES, THEY BOTH ALSO SHARED THEIR VIEWS ON THE ARTISTIC AND AESTHETIC QUALITIES OF THE WORK.

EVEN BEYOND THE EFFORTS OF THOSE PRINCIPALLY INVOLVED, THIS BOOK WOULD NOT HAVE BECOME A REALITY WITHOUT THE ASSISTANCE AND COOPERATION OF OTHER SUPPORTIVE INDIVIDUALS. WE PARTICULARLY WISH TO THANK THE FAMILY MEMBERS AND FRIENDS OF EACH OF THE PHOTOGRAPHERS. FOR ANNA CARROLL: WALTER RICH, SR., ELEANOR CARROLL DYE, AND ESPECIALLY JOHN JACKSON FOR COLLECTING AND CARING FOR THE NEGATIVES, FOR EDNA BENEDICT: HARRY BENEDICT, HOMER BENEDICT, CHRISTINA JONES, FLORENCE WHITE, AND LUKE ZILLES, THE CURRENT OWNER OF THE BENEDICT HOME WHO FOUND GLASS PLATE NEGATIVES IN HIS BASEMENT AND DONATED THEM TO DCHA, FOR LENA UNDERWOOD: KAREN AND DAVE UNDERWOOD, DAN AND BETTY UNDERWOOD, KEN AND TRUDY UNDERWOOD, AND RON BALLARD.

SEVERAL FUNDING AGENCIES HELPED BRING THIS PROJECT TO COMPLETION. THANKS GO TO THE A. LINDSAY AND OLIVE B. O'CONNOR FOUNDATION FOR SUPPORT TOWARDS THIS BOOK AND THE ACCOMPANYING EXHIBIT. THE NEW YORK STATE COUNCIL ON THE ARTS, THROUGH THE ROXBURY ARTS GROUP DECENTRALIZATION PROGRAM, HELPED BRING PUBLIC ATTENTION TO THE WORK OF LENA UNDERWOOD. THE CONSERVATION/PRESERVATION DISCRETIONARY GRANT FUND, A PART OF THE NEW YORK STATE ARCHIVES, HELPED DCHA TO RE-HOUSE, COPY, AND CARE FOR THE NEGATIVES OF EDNA BENEDICT, ORGANIZED BY BARBARA DAVIDSEN. OUR THANKS ALSO GO TO CAROL CLEMENT FOR HER BOOK DESIGN.

WE WISH TO EXPRESS VERY SPECIAL GRATITUDE TO ALL OF THE PARTICIPANTS.

JOHN T. HAMILTON, JR.
PRESIDENT
DELAWARE COUNTY HISTORICAL ASSOCIATION

Table of Contents

CHAPTER 1

PHOTOGRAPHY AS A POPULAR HOBBY

 THE JARRING SOUNDS OF TIRES SQUEALING, GLASS SHATTERING AND METAL SCRAPING METAL HAD BARELY STILLED WHEN THE PHOTOGRAPHER ARRIVED. BOX CAMERA IN HAND, SHE JOINED DOZENS OF CURIOUS BYSTANDERS WHO SURVEYED THE WRECKAGE OF FINLEY J. SHEPARD'S LOCOMOBILE, ITS FRONT END MANGLED AFTER IT HAD BEEN STRUCK BY A MILK TRAIN AND ROLLED INTO THE CROSSING NEAR MR. SHEPARD'S KIRKSIDE PARK.

THE PHOTOGRAPHER SNAPPED A FEW SHOTS AND MARVELLED THAT BOTH MR. SHEPARD AND HIS PASSENGER TAYLOR MORE SURVIVED THE COLLISION. AS THE *ROXBURY TIMES* LATER REPORTED, THE TWO MEN WERE TAKEN TO DR. JULIAN GAUL'S OFFICE BY KIRKSIDE SUPERINTENDENT J. G. LUTZ, "QUITE BADLY CUT BY GLASS FROM THE WINDSHIELD AND SOMEWHAT SHAKEN UP."

THE PHOTOS TAKEN AT THE CRASH SCENE THAT AUGUST AFTERNOON IN 1924 WERE IN SAD CONTRAST TO THOSE TAKEN EARLIER THAT SUMMER OF MR. SHEPARD IN HIS BELOVED ROADSTER, ACCOMPANIED BY ATTORNEY RALPH IVES AND CHAUFFEUR TOM PORTER AT THE WHEEL. LIKE THE PRIVATE RAILROAD CAR THE SHEPARDS ARRIVED IN EVERY SUMMER, THE LOCOMOBILE, WITH AMENITIES SUCH AS THE GOLFBAG HOLDER ATTACHED TO THE FRONT RUNNING BOARD, WAS A SYMBOL OF THE FAMILY'S WEALTH AND THE ENVY OF ROXBURYITES, WHO KEPT CAREFUL TRACK OF THE SEASONAL COMINGS AND GOINGS OF THEIR PROMINENT

NEIGHBORS. NOT LONG AFTER THE ACCIDENT, THE *TIMES* NOTED THAT "MR. AND MRS. FINLEY J. SHEPARD, CHILDREN, GUESTS, SECRETARIES, CHAUFFEURS AND SERVANTS LEFT FOR LYNDHURST AT IRVINGTON, WHERE THEY WILL SPEND A FEW MONTHS BEFORE RETURNING TO NEW YORK CITY."

WHAT HAPPENED TO FINLEY SHEPARD AND HIS LOCOMOBILE THAT HOT AUGUST DAY WAS BIG NEWS IN LITTLE ROXBURY. NOW, NEARLY 90 YEARS LATER, A SKETCHY NEWSPAPER ARTICLE—AND A PHOTOGRAPH ATTRIBUTED TO LENA BOUTON UNDERWOOD—ARE THE ONLY EVIDENCE IT EVER HAPPENED. THE RICH AND POWERFUL HAVE FADED FROM THE SCENE, THE LOCOMOBILE IS AN OBSCURE FOOTNOTE IN AUTOMOTIVE HISTORY, AND THE MILK TRAIN HAS LONG SINCE STOPPED RUMBLING THROUGH ROXBURY. BUT THE PHOTO REMAINS. THROUGH IT WE ARE OFFERED A GLIMPSE OF A TIME QUICKLY FLOWN BUT FOREVER PRESERVED.

SUCH IS THE CONTRIBUTION OF ANNA CARROLL, EDNA GEORGIA BENEDICT AND LENA BOUTON UNDERWOOD, THREE PHOTOGRAPHERS OF DELAWARE COUNTY, NEW YORK, IN THE CATSKILL MOUNTAINS, WHO SECURED FOR ALL TIME THE MEMORIES OF THEIR COMMUNITIES, APPLYING TO GLASS AND PAPER LASTING IMAGES OF THE PEOPLE, PLACES AND EVENTS THAT DEFINED THEIR LIVES.

ANNA CARROLL (1868-1925) WAS A NATIVE OF ROXBURY WHO SPENT MUCH OF HER ADULT LIFE IN HOBART. NEVER MARRIED, SHE TOOK UP PHOTOGRAPHY AS A YOUNG WOMAN. WORKING PRIMARILY FROM 1900 TO 1920, SHE PRODUCED HUNDREDS OF GLASS PLATE NEGATIVES, LARGELY CANDIDS OR INFORMALLY POSED SHOTS TAKEN IN THE HOBART, STAMFORD AND SOUTH KORTRIGHT AREAS. MOST OF HER NEGATIVES ARE NOW IN THE COLLECTION OF JOHN JACKSON OF JEFFERSON, NY.

EDNA GEORGIA BENEDICT (1888-1963) WAS BORN IN WEST MEREDITH AND TAUGHT IN SEVERAL ONE-ROOM SCHOOLS BEFORE HER MARRIAGE TO HOWARD BENEDICT IN 1913. HER COLLECTION OF NEARLY 200 GLASS PLATE NEGATIVES

SPANS THE PERIOD FROM 1904 TO 1925, AND DEPICTS LANDSCAPES, FAMILY AND FRIENDS IN THE WEST MEREDITH-TREADWELL AREA. ALL BUT ABOUT 20 OF THESE NEGATIVES ARE IN THE COLLECTION OF THE DELAWARE COUNTY HISTORICAL ASSOCIATION.

LENA BOUTON UNDERWOOD (1890-1990) SPENT ALL BUT A BRIEF PERIOD OF HER LIFE IN ROXBURY. MARRIED IN 1927 TO GEORGE UNDERWOOD, SHE WAS THE ONLY ONE OF THE THREE WOMEN PHOTOGRAPHERS PROFILED HERE TO BEAR CHILDREN. MANY OF THE 2,500 NITRATE, CELLULOSE AND SAFETY FILM NEGATIVES STILL OWNED BY HER FAMILY ARE OF THE UNDERWOODS' TWO SONS, DANIEL AND KENNETH. BUT LENA UNDERWOOD, WORKING BETWEEN THE LATE 1920S AND THE EARLY 1950S, WAS ALSO THE ONLY ONE OF THE THREE TO USE PHOTOGRAPHY AS MORE THAN A HOBBY, TAKING LICENSING PHOTOS AND DOING FILM DEVELOPING, COPY WORK AND OTHER COMMERCIAL JOBS TO HELP SUPPORT THE FAMILY DURING THE DIFFICULT DEPRESSION YEARS

UNTIL NOW, FEW OF THESE WOMEN'S PHOTOGRAPHS HAVE BEEN PUBLISHED FORMALLY. SOME OF THE CARROLL PHOTOS HAVE BEEN REPRODUCED AS POSTCARDS, OTHERS AS PRINTS FOR PRIVATE BUYERS. AS FAR AS IS KNOWN, NONE OF BENEDICT'S PHOTOGRAPHS HAVE BEEN PUBLICLY EXHIBITED. ALTHOUGH SHE DID A SIGNIFICANT AMOUNT OF COMMERCIAL WORK, ONLY ONE OF LENA UNDERWOOD'S PHOTOS, OF SON DAN MILKING A COW, IS KNOWN TO HAVE APPEARED IN PRINT—IN THE PAGES OF *LIFE MAGAZINE*, 50 YEARS AFTER SHE SNAPPED THE PHOTO IN HER BROTHER-IN-LAW'S BARN.

YET, THOUGH THEIR WORK WAS UNHERALDED, THESE WOMEN WERE PROMINENT, RESPECTED MEMBERS OF THEIR COMMUNITIES, AND THEIR SERVICES WERE APPARENTLY MUCH IN DEMAND. THEIR PHOTOGRAPHS OF SCHOOL AND CHURCH GROUPS AND SOCIAL EVENTS, OF FARM WORKERS AND CHILDREN AT PLAY, OF VILLAGE BUILDINGS AND RURAL LANDSCAPES, HELPED PROVIDE A SENSE OF

PRIDE AND COHESION AMONG COMMUNITY RESIDENTS, IN THE PROCESS CREATING A DISTINCT IDENTITY FOR THEMSELVES.

WITH CAMERA AND TRIPOD IN TOW, EARLY WOMEN PHOTOGRAPHERS GARNERED A CERTAIN AMOUNT OF INDEPENDENCE DURING THE EARLY DAYS OF THE TWENTIETH CENTURY, A PERIOD THAT WITNESSED THE STIRRINGS OF GREAT CHANGE FOR WOMEN. WOMEN HAD ALREADY GAINED NATIONAL ATTENTION FOR OUTSPOKENNESS IN TEMPERANCE CRUSADES AND OTHER NATIONAL CAUSES, FOR DARING TO WEAR BLOOMERS AND PANTS, AND FOR SMOKING, DRINKING AND OPENLY ENGAGING IN OUTINGS AND ACTIVITIES WITH MEN. WOMEN BECAME MUCH MORE PUBLIC ABOUT THEIR NEW FREEDOMS, AND WERE RECOGNIZED IN TURN-OF-THE-CENTURY MAGAZINES FOR THEIR INDEPENDENT SPIRIT AND ATHLETIC ZEAL.

IT WOULD BE INACCURATE TO SAY, HOWEVER, THAT CARROLL, BENEDICT AND UNDERWOOD DELIBERATELY SET ABOUT TO CHART NEW PATHS OF INDEPENDENCE WITH THEIR PHOTOGRAPHY. THEY WERE NOT FEMINISTS, IN MODERN-DAY TERMS. QUITE THE OPPOSITE WAS TRUE, AS THEY CHOSE SUBJECTS THAT ACTUALLY UPHELD TRADITIONAL WOMEN'S ROLES AND COMMUNITY VALUES. ANNA CARROLL'S MADONNA-LIKE PORTRAIT OF A MOTHER IN WHITE HOLDING HER ANGELIC CHILD IS A GOOD EXAMPLE OF THIS.

NONETHELESS, ALL THREE WOMEN TOOK ADVANTAGE OF THE RISING POPULARITY OF PHOTOGRAPHY TO CARVE A NICHE FOR THEMSELVES, AND TO USE IT AS A MEANS OF SELF-EXPRESSION. IT ALLOWED THEM TO STEP BEYOND CONVENTIONAL ROLES, YET RETAIN SECURITY WITHIN THEIR COMMUNITIES. GOING FURTHER, CARROLL, BENEDICT AND UNDERWOOD MAY BE CONSIDERED FOLK ARTISTS. POPULAR CULTURE HAS CREATED A LIMITED DEFINITION OF FOLK ART— QUILTS, FIDDLING AND WEATHERVANES COME TO MIND. BUT A TRUE DEFINITION OF FOLK ART CASTS A WIDER NET, AS DESCRIBED BY FOLKLORIST DOUGLAS DENATALE: "EACH COMMUNITY HAS ITS ARTISTS—THOSE INDIVIDUALS WHO ARE ABLE TO MOVE

BEYOND EVERYDAY NEEDS AND GIVE VOICE TO THE COMMUNITY'S GREATEST CONCERNS; TO BRING COMMONPLACE METHODS [SUCH AS PHOTOGRAPHY] TO THEIR FULLEST REALIZATION; OR TO GIVE BACK TO THE COMMUNITY AN IMAGE OF ITSELF."

CLEARLY, ALL THREE OF THE WOMEN CONSIDERED HERE REFLECTED THE AESTHETICS OF THEIR COMMUNITIES, WHERE THEIR WORK WAS ACCEPTED AND WHERE THEY ACHIEVED A CERTAIN STATUS. THEIR WORK INDICATED CONSCIOUS AESTHETIC CHOICES, REFINED OVER TIME AND COMBINED WITH MASTERY OF WHAT WAS THEN A DIFFICULT TECHNICAL MEDIUM. THESE WOMEN STRUGGLED TO DEVELOP THEIR ART INDEPENDENTLY OF ANY FORMAL EDUCATIONAL PROCESS— ANOTHER DEFINITION OF FOLK ART—HAVING BEEN EITHER SELF-TAUGHT, OR GUIDED BY ANOTHER MEMBER OF THE COMMUNITY. THEY LEARNED PHOTOGRAPHY IN MUCH THE SAME WAY THAT LOCAL QUILTERS LEARNED TO QUILT, OR WOODCARVERS TO CARVE.

ALTHOUGH PHOTOGRAPHY IS A MECHANICAL PROCESS, THE WORK CONSIDERED IN THIS BOOK IS HARDLY OF THE 'POINT AND SHOOT' VARIETY. CARROLL, BENEDICT AND UNDERWOOD CONTROLLED EVERY ASPECT OF THE PROCESS, INCLUDING DEVELOPING THEIR OWN FILM AND PRINTING THEIR OWN PHOTOGRAPHS. THEIR COMMITMENT TO PHOTOGRAPHY, THEIR METHODS OF LIFE-LONG LEARNING, THEIR INVOLVEMENT IN AND DEEP RESPONSE TO COMMUNITY AND ITS AESTHETICS, ALLOW US TO CONSIDER THEM AS "FOLK ARTISTS."

FOR PHOTOGRAPHERS SUCH AS CARROLL, BENEDICT AND UNDERWOOD, THE TAKING OF IMAGES WAS NOT AN ISOLATED ACTIVITY—IT WAS AS MUCH A RESPONSE TO EVENTS IN AND AROUND THEIR LIVES AS IT WAS A DESIRE TO ADOPT A NEW LEISURE-TIME ACTIVITY. AND WHILE THEY BECAME IDENTIFIED WITH THEIR CAMERAS, NONE OF THESE WOMEN EMPHASIZED THE TAKING OF PICTURES OVER ANY OTHER PART OF THEIR LIVES. THEY DID NOT LET PHOTOGRAPHY REPLACE THEIR DUTIES TO HOME OR COMMUNITY. RAISED ON FARMS, CARROLL, BENEDICT

AND UNDERWOOD ASCRIBED TO THE TRADITIONAL WOMAN'S ROLE AS THE KEEPER OF A CLEAN, PEACEFUL HOME, NURTURER OF HAPPY, HEALTHY CHILDREN, HELPMATE TO ONE'S PARTNER AND PURVEYOR OF MORAL AND SPIRITUAL GUIDANCE.

CARROLL HAD NO HUSBAND OR CHILDREN, BUT CARED FOR HER AGED MOTHER, AND, LIKE EDNA BENEDICT WHO ALSO REMAINED CHILDLESS, SHOWERED AFFECTION AND ATTENTION ON NIECES AND NEPHEWS. CHILDREN CAME RELATIVELY LATE IN LIFE FOR LENA UNDERWOOD, WHO ALSO CARED FOR AN AGED AUNT AND UNCLE. "HOME CAME FIRST FOR MOM," RECALLS SON DAN.

ALL THREE WOMEN WERE VERY ACTIVE IN THEIR RESPECTIVE CHURCHES, AND REFLECTED THE INTERESTS OF OTHER RURAL WOMEN BY PARTICIPATING IN COMMUNITY ACTIVITIES. "THE LADIES [OF THE WILLING WORKERS OF WEST MEREDITH] MET ONCE A MONTH TO VISIT, TIE OFF QUILTS, AND DO OTHER PROJECTS TO HELP ONE ANOTHER," REMEMBERED EDNA BENEDICT'S NIECE, CHRISTINA JONES. "THEY MET IN HOMES, AND AUNT EDNA ENTERTAINED THE GROUP SOMETIMES. THIS WAS AN OCCASION FOR GETTING THE CAMERA OUT!"

PERHAPS BENEDICT WAS THERE WITH HER CAMERA WHEN, ON MARCH 17, 1911, THERE WAS A "WARM SUGAR SOCIAL" AT THE TREADWELL METHODIST CHURCH, OR IN SEPTEMBER OF THAT YEAR, WHEN SEVERAL YOUNG PEOPLE GATHERED AT THE GEORGIA HOMESTEAD FOR A FRIDAY EVENING CORN ROAST. SUCH COMMUNITY-SANCTIONED OUTINGS WERE A WAY FOR BOYS AND GIRLS TO SOCIALIZE, PERHAPS TO CEMENT BONDS THAT WOULD LEAD TO MARRIAGE.

EXCEPT FOR THE VERY WEALTHY, PHOTOGRAPHY HAD TAKEN THE PLACE OF PAINTED PORTRAITS TO COMMEMORATE FAMILY MEMBERS BY THE LATE 1800S. PHOTOGRAPHY, WHICH WAS EASY TO LEARN AND YIELDED QUICKER, TRUER RESULTS, BECAME AN EASY, INEXPENSIVE ALTERNATIVE FOR MOST FAMILIES. PHOTOGRAPHERS, BOTH AMATEUR AND PROFESSIONAL, TOOK THE PLACE OF THE

ARTISTS WHO HAD PREVIOUSLY RENDERED PORTRAITS IN OIL, AND THE THREE WOMEN CONSIDERED HERE TOOK THEIR PLACE AMONG THEM.

CARROLL, BENEDICT AND UNDERWOOD BROUGHT THE FORMAL PHOTOGRAPHIC STUDIO TO THE DOORSTEPS OF COMMUNITIES WHICH HAD NONE. WHETHER IT WAS A BACKYARD, A PORCH OR A PARLOR, THE RITUAL OF HAVING A PHOTOGRAPH TAKEN WAS MADE MORE FAMILIAR, MORE IMMEDIATE—BUT NO LESS IMPORTANT.

FAMILY PHOTOS WERE KEPT WITH PRIDE, OFTEN IN PHOTOGRAPH ALBUMS, WHICH PUT EVENTS AND PEOPLE INTO ORDERLY CONTEXT. AT THE TURN OF THE CENTURY, PHOTO AND POSTCARD ALBUMS WERE A POPULAR GIFT TO GIVE A YOUNG WOMAN. BOTH EDNA BENEDICT AND LENA UNDERWOOD CREATED ALBUMS OF THEIR OWN PHOTOGRAPHS. BENEDICT'S IS REMEMBERED BY HER NIECE AS HAVING "LETTERS CUT OUT ON VELVET COVERS." IN 1922, WHEN ROLL FILM, INEXPENSIVE CAMERAS AND OUTSIDE PROCESSING HAD PUT THE CRAFT OF PHOTOGRAPHY WITHIN REACH OF MANY, MERRILL AND HUMPHRIES OF DELHI ADVERTISED "SNAP SHOT ALBUMS," CLAIMING "A PICTURE WORTH TAKING IS A PICTURE WORTH KEEPING."

MANY WOMEN, LIKE CARROLL, BENEDICT AND UNDERWOOD, EMBRACED NOT ONLY PHOTOGRAPH ALBUMS, BUT THE VERY CRAFT OF PHOTOGRAPHY. A MRS. E. A. CORWIN, IN A 1910 ISSUE OF CAMERACRAFT, DESCRIBED HER FEELINGS FOR "MY LITTLE KODAK, MY FRIEND, COMPANION AND SERVITOR," AFFECTIONATELY RECALLING "THE AFTERTIME, [WHEN] I COLLECT ABOUT ME THE CIRCLE OF SCENES AND FACES THAT HEART AND MIND SO TREASURE, DESPITE THEIR UNIMPORTANCE AND THEIR FLEETING NATURE, THOUGHTS OF HOME AND FRIENDS. . ."

NEITHER ANNA CARROLL, EDNA BENEDICT NOR LENA UNDERWOOD PRESERVED IN WORDS THEIR FEELINGS FOR THEIR CRAFT. BUT, IN SENSITIVE, BEAUTIFULLY RENDERED PHOTOGRAPHS THEY LEFT US VISUAL DIARIES THAT EVOKE THE ESSENCE OF DELAWARE COUNTY LIFE IN THE FIRST HALF OF THE TWENTIETH CENTURY.

CHAPTER 2

A BUCOLIC BACKDROP:

RURAL LIFE IN THE EARLY TWENTIETH CENTURY

AT THE TURN OF THE CENTURY, DELAWARE COUNTY WAS FARM COUNTRY. MOST OF THE 46,413 PEOPLE WHO LIVED IN THE COUNTY IN THE YEAR 1900 OCCUPIED SMALL FAMILY FARMS OR RESIDED IN THE BUSTLING HAMLETS THAT SERVED AS TRADING CENTERS FOR THOSE FARMS.

DAIRYING WAS THE PRINCIPAL INDUSTRY FROM THE LATE NINETEENTH THROUGH MUCH OF THE TWENTIETH CENTURY. MILK, BUTTER, CHEESE AND OTHER DAIRY PRODUCTS FOUND A READY MARKET BOTH LOCALLY AND IN THE DISTANT NEW YORK CITY METROPOLITAN AREA, AS FARMERS BROUGHT THEIR MILK TO CREAMERIES SPACED ALONG THE ULSTER & DELAWARE RAILROAD LINE. IN 1886, FOR EXAMPLE, THE *DELAWARE GAZETTE* REPORTED THAT MORE THAN 150 CANS OF MILK WERE BEING SHIPPED DAILY FROM HOBART TO NEW YORK CITY.

THIS REPRESENTED AN IMPORTANT SOURCE OF INCOME TO DELAWARE COUNTY FARM FAMILIES AND TO THE COMMUNITIES WHERE MUCH OF THAT MONEY WAS SPENT. IN THE EARLY YEARS OF THIS CENTURY, FOR INSTANCE, TREADWELL BOASTED THREE GENERAL STORES, A BAKERY, TOBACCO AND CONFECTIONERY STORE, HARNESS SHOP, MILLINERY STORE, EIGHT DRESSMAKERS, TWO COOPERAGES AND FOUR BLACKSMITHS. STILL, FARM FAMILIES WERE AN INDEPENDENT LOT, GROWING AND MAKING MUCH OF WHAT THEY NEEDED TO SURVIVE.

Subsistence farming was the way of life in this region when the first settlers arrived from downstate New York and New England around 1790. They found a region of stony fields and rolling, wooded hillsides, framed by the East and West Branches of the Delaware River. Tucked into a corner of the state bounded by the Hudson River on the East and the Pennsylvania state line on the west, Delaware County's topography produced a collection of insular, if not isolated communities that dotted the map over a sprawling area the size of Rhode Island.

Most farmers grew buckwheat, rye, oats, corn, potatoes and other vegetables, as well as fruit for pie and cider, and flax for linen. They found the area's hardscrabble meadows and valley pastures best suited to sheep rather than cattle, and woolen mills were developed along the many streams and rivers. Indeed, Delaware County was at one time the leading wool producer in the state. But because agriculture was not easy in this rough country, its people turned to other sources of income—bluestone, animal pelts, hemlock bark for the tanning industry, and, of course, the water all around which powered its many mills.

After the Civil War, improved breeds of dairy cattle began to gain favor with the region's farmers, and small dairy herds supplanted flocks of sheep. Delaware County became known far and wide for its rich milk and high-quality butter. Its farms captured national and international agricultural awards. Meridale Farms, one of the largest and most commercial of the county's farming operations, was established in 1888. Famous for its top quality Jersey herd, it attracted buyers from throughout the nation and abroad to its annual

LIVESTOCK SHOW AND SALE. THE NATION'S FIRST COMMERCIAL MILK PASTEURIZATION PLANT, ESTABLISHED IN 1893, WAS THE SHEFFIELD FARMS CREAMERY IN BLOOMVILLE.

ASIDE FROM DAIRYING, DELAWARE COUNTY'S RESIDENTS RAISED POULTRY, MADE CIDER AND MAPLE SYRUP, HARVESTED TIMBER, BLUESTONE AND ICE, GREW CAULIFLOWER AS A CASH CROP AND ENGAGED IN OTHER ENTERPRISES TO EARN MONEY FOR HOUSEHOLD SUPPLIES, FARM EQUIPMENT AND FOOD STAPLES THEY COULD NOT PRODUCE THEMSELVES. SOME MEN, PARTICULARLY LOGGERS AND QUARRYMEN, HIRED OUT THEIR SERVICES, PROVIDING WORK TO OTHERS. MEN LIKE ROBERT NEWMAN OF MERIDALE, WHO WAS DESCRIBED IN THE FEBRUARY 19, 1908 *STAMFORD MIRROR-RECORDER* TO HAVE "TAKEN THE JOB OF CUTTING 1,000 CORDS OF WOOD FOR DELOS MACKEY ON HIS FARM IN HOUGHTALING HOLLOW. HE HAS 15 MEN AT WORK."

HAMLETS, WITH THEIR MILLS, SHOPS AND SERVICES, DEVELOPED ALONG VALLEY WATERWAYS TO MEET THE COMMERCIAL AND SOCIAL NEEDS OF THEIR OUTLYING NEIGHBORS. *SPAULDING'S 1896 BUSINESS DIRECTORY OF DELAWARE COUNTY* SHOWS 36 RETAIL, SERVICE AND PROFESSIONAL ENTERPRISES IN ROXBURY, 35 IN FRANKLIN AND 40 IN HOBART. THEY RANGED FROM WATCHMAKERS AND STOCK DEALERS TO DRUGGISTS, CLOTHING STORES AND HOTELS.

INDEED, THE TOURIST TRADE BECAME AN IMPORTANT PART OF THE LOCAL ECONOMY WITH THE ARRIVAL OF THE RAILROAD IN THE 1870S. ROXBURY AND HOBART WERE BUSY STOPS ON THE ULSTER & DELAWARE RAILROAD, AND MANY HOTELS AND BOARDING HOUSES ACCOMMODATED THE INFLUX OF SUMMER VISITORS FROM NEW YORK CITY AND ELSEWHERE.

ANNA CARROLL, EDNA BENEDICT AND LENA UNDERWOOD REFLECTED THESE COMMUNITY DISTINCTIONS IN THEIR PHOTOGRAPHY. UNDERWOOD AND

CARROLL WERE VILLAGE RESIDENTS, AS WERE MANY OF THEIR SUBJECTS. UNDERWOOD TOOK ADVANTAGE OF THE TOURIST TRADE IN ROXBURY TO PROCESS ROLLS OF FILM FOR SUMMER GUESTS. SHE PHOTOGRAPHED COMMUNITY ACTIVITIES, AND VILLAGE BUILDINGS, INCLUDING THE INTERIORS OF SID'S SODA SHOPPE, THE ROXBURY HOTEL AND THE GOULD CHURCH. CARROLL'S IMAGES INCLUDE A STREET SCENE OF DOWNTOWN HOBART, SHOWING HER BROTHER ARNOLD'S HARDWARE STORE, A PHOTO OF A POPULAR LOCAL CROQUET COURT AND ANOTHER OF A HOBART PARADE.

BENEDICT'S PHOTOGRAPHS ARE ALMOST EXCLUSIVELY OF PEOPLE AT WORK OR PLAY ON FARMS OR OTHER LOCATIONS IN MORE ISOLATED WEST MEREDITH. THE MILL POND, THE CREAMERY AND THE WAGON HOUSE WERE AMONG HER SUBJECTS. HER PORTRAIT OF A YOUNG MAN POSING AMID A FIELD OF NEW-MOWN HAY, AND A PHOTOGRAPH OF HUSBAND HOWARD AT WORK AT A GRINDSTONE IN THE SHADE OF A MAPLE TREE ARE GOOD EXAMPLES OF HER WORK.

ALL THREE WOMEN WERE PRODUCTS OF FARM COUNTRY, INFLUENCED BY THEIR RURAL UPBRINGINGS AND BY THE PROXIMITY TO FRIENDS AND FAMILY MEMBERS WHO REMAINED ON THE FARM. LENA UNDERWOOD TOOK MANY PHOTOS ON HER BROTHER-IN-LAW'S FARM, WHERE HER FAMILY OFTEN VISITED FOR WORK OR PLAY. ONE OF ANNA CARROLL'S MOST APPEALING SHOTS DEPICTS TWO YOUNG GIRLS, ETHEL AND GRACE KENNEY, AT A COMMON ACTIVITY ON FARMSTEADS— FEEDING THE CHICKENS.

TOO, THE PHOTOGRAPHS OF ALL THREE WOMEN TEND TO UPHOLD THE IMAGE OF FEMALE VIRTUE AND DUTY. DESPITE THE DEVELOPMENT OF ELECTRICITY AND INDOOR PLUMBING, AND THE ADVENT OF NEW DEVICES LIKE WASHING MACHINES AND VACUUM SWEEPERS, THE WORK OF RURAL WOMEN WAS DIFFICULT AND TIME-CONSUMING, EVEN DANGEROUS. NEWSPAPERS REGULARLY REPORTED BROKEN ARMS SUFFERED BY WOMEN WHOSE SLEEVES BECAME CAUGHT IN

WASHING-MACHINE WRINGERS, OR BURNS CAUSED BY CLOTHING IGNITED BY GREASE ON THE STOVE, AS WAS THE CASE IN HOBART IN 1900 WHEN DORA VROOMAN WAS BADLY INJURED.

WASHING, IRONING AND MENDING CLOTHES FOR THE FAMILY, GARDENING, BAKING AND PRESERVING PRODUCE, CLEANING THE HOUSE AND TENDING THE CHILDREN MEANT WOMEN WORKED FROM DAWN UNTIL LONG AFTER DARK. AN EARLY DIARY WRITTEN BY ELIZA MEAD OF WALTON PAINTS A PICTURE OF WHAT LIFE WAS LIKE FOR WOMEN, AND THOUGH IT WAS WRITTEN IN 1860, IT MIGHT HAVE BEEN PENNED FIFTY YEARS LATER. "SATURDAY, JULY 7. CHURNED AND PACKED DOWN 77 LB. OF BUTTER. JAMES HELPED ME WASH 2 BED QUILTS AND A PIECE OF WOOL THAT WAS SHEARED LAST YEAR. THE QUILTS ARE DRY AND IN THE HOUSE. THE WOOL IS OUT YET. BAKED CAKE AND MADE PUDDING FOR LUNCH TOMORROW AND MOPPED. GOT THROUGH JUST BEFORE DINNER. HAVE FINISHED THE DRESS AND MADE A POCKET HANDKERCHIEF OUT OF LINEN PHOEBE SENT."

THE HOME WAS THE CENTER OF THE UNIVERSE FOR MOST WOMEN OF THE TIME. "A CLEAN, FRESH, AND WELL-ORDERED HOUSE EXERCISES OVER ITS INMATES A MORAL, NO LESS A PHYSICAL INFLUENCE, AND HAS A DIRECT TENDENCY TO MAKE MEMBERS OF THE FAMILY SOBER, PEACEABLE AND CONSIDERATE OF THE FEELINGS AND HAPPINESS OF EACH OTHER," EXPLAINED AN 1883 GUIDE, *OUR HOMES AND HOW TO MAKE THEM HEALTHY*.

FEMALES IN THE VICTORIAN ERA WERE ALSO TAUGHT THAT A CLEAN AND BEAUTIFULLY DECORATED HOME WAS A SYMBOL OF THEIR WORTH AND PRODUCTIVITY; IT REFLECTED THE TRUE NATURE OF THE WOMAN OF THE HOUSE. AND WOMEN RECEIVED PLENTY OF DIRECTIVES ON HOW BEST TO EXHIBIT THEIR BELONGINGS. TAKE FOR EXAMPLE, A PUBLICATION ISSUED BY THE NEW YORK STATE COLLEGE OF AGRICULTURE AT CORNELL IN 1915, WHICH EXPLAINED THE PROPER WAY TO ARRANGE HOME FURNISHINGS: "SYSTEM, ORDER, CLASSIFICATION

AND COMMON SENSE SHOULD BE TAKEN BY THE HOUSEWIFE AS THE BASIS OF ARRANGEMENT OF ALL FURNISHINGS IN THE HOME, FROM THE FURNITURE IN THE LIVING ROOM, TO THE CONTENTS OF THE JELLY CLOSET."

A PHOTOGRAPH OF A PARLOR TAKEN BY EDNA BENEDICT SHOWED MANY ASPECTS OF WHAT WAS CONSIDERED TASTEFUL, STYLISH INTERIOR DECORATION OF THE EARLY 1900S: AN IVY PLANT SPREADS OVER THE FLOOR, AROUND AN ANCESTRAL PORTRAIT DISPLAYED ON AN EASEL, AND UP TO THE WALLPAPERED CEILING.

EVEN A WOMAN'S LEISURE TIME WAS LARGELY SPENT IN HOME-BEAUTIFICATION PROJECTS, SUCH AS CRAFTS AND NEEDLEWORK. ANNA CARROLL'S INTERIOR PHOTOGRAPH OF A BEDROOM SHOWS MANY SUCH OBJECTS—A WOODBURNT WASTEBASKET, EMBROIDERED RUNNERS ON THE DRESSER AND TABLE, AND SEVERAL HAND-MADE MOTTOS. ONE OF EDNA BENEDICT'S PHOTOGRAPHS SHOWS A GROUP OF FOUR WOMEN, OBVIOUSLY ENJOYING A SUMMER OUTING BY A STREAM, SEATED ON A FALLEN LOG. TWO OF THEM HAVE BROUGHT THEIR KNITTING.

CARROLL, BENEDICT AND UNDERWOOD THEMSELVES FOUND IT DIFFICULT TO SQUEEZE PHOTOGRAPHY INTO THEIR BUSY DAYS. RECALLS KEN UNDERWOOD OF HIS MOTHER, "SHE SPENT MOST OF HER TIME HOUSEKEEPING, GARDENING, CANNING, PRESERVING. THEN SHE'D GET FIDGETY WITH THE FILM PILING UP, SO SHE'D TAKE A DAY OFF AND DO THEM."

BENEDICT'S NIECE, CHRISTINA BLACKMER JONES, RELATES THAT HER AUNT "WAS AN ARDENT FOOD PRESERVER. SHE MADE PIES, JAMS AND JELLIES FROM BLUEBERRIES, BLACKBERRIES, ELDERBERRIES AND STRAWBERRIES. AND SHE CANNED MEAT, TOO. IT WAS USUALLY A BUTCHERED COW FROM THE HERD."

MUCH OF THE WORK—AND PLAY—OF BOTH WOMEN AND MEN WAS SHARED WITH NEIGHBORS AND FRIENDS. THE WORK OF BRINGING IN THE CROPS OR

BUILDING BARNS WAS MADE EASIER WITH THE HELP OF FARM NEIGHBORS, WHO THEN SHARED FOOD, MUSIC AND FUN IN COMMUNAL RELAXATION. ALEX NICHOL, A HAMDEN FARMER WRITING IN HIS DIARY AUGUST 11, 1906, RELATED THIS: "MILO TOOK THE MILK. WE WENT ON THE HILL AND SPLIT WOOD UNTIL 10 A.M., CAME HOME AND TO A PICNIC OVER AT TRACY BLANCHARD'S. ROB RODE PRINCE AND WE DROVE FLOSS. THERE WAS A LARGE CROWD, 32 NUMBERS AT THE PLATFORM DANCE." MR. NICHOL REPORTED ANOTHER PICNIC ON AUGUST 22, WHEN 127 PEOPLE ATTENDED, AND AN ICE-CREAM-MAKING PARTY WITH A NEIGHBOR FAMILY ON AUGUST 23. BUT MOST ACCOUNTS DETAILED WORK, WORK AND MORE WORK, MOST OF IT, LIKE THE FUN AND THE SORROW OF THEIR LIVES, SHARED: "TUESDAY, SEPT. 4, 1906. ROB WENT UP AND HELPED FYFFES CUT THEIR BUCKWHEAT IN THE FORENOON. THEY ALL CAME OVER AND WE WENT ON OUR HILL AND RAKED THE LAST OF OUR OATS AND DREW THEM IN TWO BIG LOADS...SEPTEMBER 1, 1911. I TOOK THE MILK. SOLD A BUSHEL OF PEARS TO MRS. DANIELS, $1.00. WE PICKED THE PEARS AND PLUMS. WE WENT ON THE HILL AFTER NOON AND CUT LUMBER FOR FENCE POSTS."

COUNTRY PEOPLE AND THEIR SMALL-TOWN NEIGHBORS MADE HOSPITALITY A DELAWARE COUNTY STANDARD. THE "WHOLESOME SOCIAL ATMOSPHERE, HIGH MORAL TONE AND READY HOSPITALITY" OF HOBART WERE TOUTED BY THAT TOWN'S CITIZENS' ASSOCIATION IN A 1913 PROMOTIONAL BOOKLET. "THE CHURCHES ARE ACTIVELY REPRESENTED BY THEIR SOCIAL AND AID SOCIETIES. THE WOMEN'S CIVIC CLUB AND THE CITIZENS' ASSOCIATION HAVE AN ACTIVE COMBINED MEMBERSHIP OF NEARLY 150 AND BOTH ORGANIZATIONS EXERT A SPLENDID INFLUENCE OVER THE COMMUNITY. . . HOBART HAS FOUR FRATERNAL ORGANIZATIONS, ALL DOING ACTIVE WORK. THEY ARE ST. ANDREW'S LODGE, NO. 289; F.& A.M.L.; HOBART LODGE, NO. 63, I.O.O.F.; HOBART VALLEY LODGE OF REBEKAHS, NO. 470; AND BOY SCOUTS OF AMERICA."

Church suppers, sleighing parties, ice cream socials, quilting bees, choir singing and house dances were traditional social activities of farm and town dwellers, and the subject of many a photograph. A typical notice in the *Roxbury Times* February 22, 1930 announced a chicken pie dinner to be hosted by the Bag and Quilt Committees of the Social Society at the Gould Memorial Reformed Church. The menu included chicken pie, mashed potatoes, carrots and peas, fruit jello, mince pie and tapioca pudding, and the cost was 50 cents a plate. "The dinner will be served at noon so the children will be able to eat, also all men are welcome in their work clothes," the article noted. The Social Society took pains to accommodate working men (the federal census counted nearly 4,000 farms in Delaware County that year) and village schoolchildren.

At that time, before school centralization went into effect, students who lived outside villages usually attended one-room schools. A single teacher would instruct children in grades one through eight, the older children often coaching the younger ones (when they weren't kept home to help with farm chores). Clara Stewart, in her history of School District #2 in the Town of Meredith, noted that instruction in the "Three Rs"—readin', 'ritin' and 'rithmetic—was provided so that farm dwellers would at least have a basic education, enabling them to read the Bible, figure their mortgage and taxes, and communicate.

School was usually called at 9 a.m., Clara Stewart relates. Classes would be 10 to 20 minutes long, depending on the number of grades and the number of children in each grade. Classes were

CONDUCTED FROM FIRST THROUGH EIGHTH GRADE, AND THOSE GOING FURTHER WOULD ENTER AN ACADEMY OR APPRENTICESHIP.

TEACHERS WOULD WALK, RIDE HORSES OR BICYCLES OR TAKE THE TRAIN TO SCHOOL. MANY BOARDED WITH DISTRICT FAMILIES. STUDENTS HELPED BRING IN WOOD FOR THE STOVE AND WATER FROM A NEARBY WELL OR SPRING. THERE WERE USUALLY TWO RECESSES, ONE IN MID-MORNING AND ONE IN MID-AFTERNOON, AND A BREAK FOR LUNCH, WHEN YOUNGSTERS WOULD OFTEN PLAY GAMES LIKE "KICK THE BUCKET," "TISKET-A-TASKET," "I SPY," "SNAP THE WHIP," "POM-POM PULLAWAY," AND "FOX AND GEESE." MANY FORMER STUDENTS OF THE ONE-ROOM SCHOOL, WHICH PREDOMINATED IN DELAWARE COUNTY INTO THE 1930S AND '40S, STILL RECALL THE SOUND OF THE HAND BELL TEACHERS USED TO CALL THEM IN FROM PLAY.

EDNA BENEDICT TAUGHT IN THREE SUCH SCHOOLS BEFORE SHE WAS MARRIED, AND IN 1905 PHOTOGRAPHED THE STUDENTS OF THE PINES SCHOOL IN WEST MEREDITH. IN THE CLASS WERE HER BROTHER, WENDELL GEORGIA, AND TWO BROTHERS OF HER FUTURE HUSBAND, HARRY AND HOMER BENEDICT. RECALLED HARRY: "OUR ATTENDANCE WOULD RUN AROUND 15 AVERAGE. IN WINTER, SOME OF THE LARGER BOYS WOULD COME AND WE'D GET UP TO MAYBE 25. WE HAD DOUBLE BENCHES THAT HELD TWO IN A SEAT, WITH A SLOPED WOODEN TOP MADE OF PINE AND EASY TO CARVE. THOSE BOYS WOULD CARVE LITTLE GROOVES IN A ROW OR MAYBE A SQUARE AND RUN A SLOT THROUGH THEM WITH A PENCIL. AND EVERY DESK WAS ALIKE. WHILE I WAS STILL THERE, THEY PUT IN ALL NEW DESKS, SINGLE ONES, BOUGHT FROM SEARS AND ROEBUCK."

THE PINES SCHOOL, DISTRICT# 7, RECEIVED ITS NAME FROM THE PINES CREAMERY, WHICH HAD OPENED SHORTLY BEFORE THE SCHOOL WAS BUILT. MOST OF THE TREES IN THE AREA WERE OAK OR PINE (HENCE THE NAME FOR THE

CREAMERY AND SCHOOL), AND THE SCHOOLHOUSE HELD A SPECIAL TRIBUTE TO THE AREA'S NATURAL HERITAGE—ACORNS AND OAK LEAVES WERE CARVED ON THE VERGE BOARD BENEATH THE GABLED OVERHANG.

TO BECOME A TEACHER, BENEDICT HAD EARLIER ATTENDED THE DELAWARE LITERARY INSTITUTE IN FRANKLIN, WHERE SHE MAY VERY WELL HAVE PICKED UP HER INTEREST IN PHOTOGRAPHY, AN INTEREST SHE MAINTAINED FOR THE NEXT HALF-CENTURY.

BENEDICT, AND HER COLLEAGUES LENA UNDERWOOD AND ANNA CARROLL, USED THEIR CRAFT TO RECORD THE ACTIVITIES OF THE PEOPLE AROUND THEM, AND TO RENDER PERMANENT SOMETHING OF THEIR LIVES AND TIMES. BUT A DEEPER MOTIVATION WAS LIKELY AT WORK. IT WAS SUCCINCTLY EXPRESSED BY GERTRUDE KASEBIER, A WIFE AND MOTHER OF THREE WHO WENT FROM AMATEUR PHOTOGRAPHER TO OPENING HER OWN PHOTOGRAPHY STUDIO IN NEW YORK CITY IN 1897: "IT IS NOT JUST THAT I AM ANXIOUS TO MAKE THESE PHOTOGRAPHS FOR THE SAKE OF THE PEOPLE. I AM THIRSTY TO DO IT FOR MY OWN SAKE, TO EXPRESS WHAT THERE IS IN ME."

CHAPTER 3

BEHIND THE CAMERA:

WOMEN AS PHOTOGRAPHERS

 THE RISE OF PHOTOGRAPHY AS A POPULAR FORM OF SOCIAL RECREATION AND A MEANS OF SELF-EXPRESSION FOR WOMEN WAS A RESULT OF THREE THINGS: THE DEVELOPMENT OF CAMERAS THAT WERE EASIER TO USE, THE AVAILABILITY OF DEVELOPING AND PRINTING SERVICES, AND THE WIDESPREAD USE OF ADVERTISING AIMED AT PERSUADING WOMEN THAT PHOTOGRAPHY WAS AN ACTIVITY WELL SUITED TO THEIR FEMININE VIRTUES.

THE ADVENT OF THE FOLDING BOX CAMERA AND ROLL FILM IN THE LATE 1880S MADE PHOTOGRAPHY ACCESSIBLE TO ANYONE WITH A FEW DOLLARS WHO WISHED TO USE THE NEW TECHNOLOGY TO RECORD THE EVENTS OF THEIR LIVES. THE CAMERAS WERE MORE PORTABLE THAN THE HEAVIER GLASS PLATE CAMERAS, THEIR USE WAS AS SIMPLE AS THE CLICK OF A BUTTON, AND THEY OPERATED AT FASTER SPEEDS, WHICH IN MOST CASES ELIMINATED THE NECESSITY OF TRIPODS.

ALTHOUGH WOMEN WERE NOT THE SOLE TARGETS OF PHOTOGRAPHY'S PROMOTERS (GEORGE EASTMAN TOUTED IT AS A HOBBY FOR "ANYBODY AND EVERYBODY," INCLUDING "BICYCLISTS AND BOATING MEN, ARTISTS, SURGEONS, SPORTSMEN AND CAMPING PARTIES, ENGINEERS AND ARCHITECTS, AND LOVERS OF FINE ANIMALS"), MANY ARTICLES AND ADVERTISEMENTS IN PHOTOGRAPHY MAGAZINES IN THE LATE NINETEENTH AND EARLY TWENTIETH CENTURIES ENCOURAGED WOMEN—IN PARTICULAR MIDDLE-CLASS WOMEN OF LEISURE—TO

TAKE UP THE HOBBY. "I BELIEVE THERE IS NO OTHER VOCATION OPEN TO WOMEN, IN WHICH SO MUCH OF THE PLEASURE AND PROFIT IS COMBINED WITH SO LITTLE DRUDGERY AS THAT OF PHOTOGRAPHY," SAID ELIZABETH FLINT WADE IN AN ARTICLE TITLED, "PHOTOGRAPHY THROUGH WOMEN'S EYES," PUBLISHED IN THE JUNE, 1894 ISSUE OF *THE PHOTO-AMERICAN*.

INDEED, WOMEN WERE THOUGHT TO POSSESS PERSONAL CHARACTERISTICS THAT MADE THEM PARTICULARLY GOOD AT THE CRAFT. SAID RICHARD HINES, JR. IN AN 1898 ADDRESS BEFORE THE MOBILE, ALABAMA ART LEAGUE, "CLEANLINESS AND PATIENCE ARE TWO OF THE CARDINAL VIRTUES NECESSARY TO THE SUCCESSFUL PURSUIT OF PHOTOGRAPHY. THE LIGHT, DELICATE TOUCH OF A WOMAN, THE EYE FOR LIGHT AND SHADE, TOGETHER WITH THEIR ARTISTIC PERCEPTION, RENDER THEM PECULIARLY FITTED TO SUCCEED IN THIS WORK."

AS RECREATIONAL PHOTOGRAPHY GREW IN POPULARITY, CAMERA COMPANIES USED WOMEN IN THEIR ADVERTISEMENTS TO PROVE THAT THIS WAS AN EASY AND ENJOYABLE HOBBY. THE EASTMAN KODAK COMPANY BECAME KNOWN FOR ITS KODAK GIRL TRADEMARK, WHICH EMERGED IN 1901. THE KODAK GIRL, ALWAYS SHOWN WITH HER FOLDING CAMERA, PROMOTED THE FUN AND VERSATILITY OF PHOTOGRAPHY. SIMPLICITY AND FASHION WERE SHOWN AS THE HALLMARKS OF KODAK CAMERAS.

WOMEN IN THESE ADVERTISEMENTS WERE SEEN AS ADVENTURESOME, FREEDOM-LOVING AND INTERESTED IN THE WORLD AROUND THEM. THE KODAK GIRL USED BY THE BRITISH-BASED KODAK LTD., EASILY RECOGNIZABLE IN HER STRIPED DRESS, WAS THE FIRM'S CALLING CARD FOR MORE THAN 30 YEARS. FULL-SIZE CUT-OUT FIGURES OF THE KODAK GIRL WERE GIVEN TO DEALERS FOR DISPLAY, AND LIVE KODAK GIRLS ATTENDED PHOTO SHOWS AND EXHIBITIONS. THE KODAK GIRL WAS SHOWN IN SETTINGS AS DIVERSE AS AFRICA AND THE FAR EAST, BEARING A SIMPLE MESSAGE, "NO HOLIDAY IS COMPLETE WITHOUT A KODAK CAMERA."

PHOTOGRAPHY WAS THUS DEPICTED AS A MEANS OF ESCAPE FROM THE REPETITIVE TASKS OF MAINTAINING A HOME AND REARING CHILDREN.

NOR WAS THE TECHNOLOGY INVOLVED IN THE MORE ARDUOUS GLASS PLATE METHOD OF PHOTOGRAPHY, FAVORED BY ANNA CARROLL AND EDNA BENEDICT, SEEN AS A DETERRENT TO WOMEN. AN 1887 ARTICLE IN *THE LADIES MANUAL OF ART* OUTLINED "HOW TO MAKE PHOTOGRAPHS BY THE GELATIN DRY-PLATE PROCESS," AND IN 1894, *THE PHOTO-AMERICAN* ISSUED A CHALLENGE TO WOMEN TO WRITE IN ABOUT THEIR PHOTOGRAPHIC EXPERIENCES TO DISPEL THE NOTION THAT WOMEN WERE NOT DEDICATED TO THE PROCESSES OR TOUGH ENOUGH TO HANDLE THE EQUIPMENT OR CHEMICALS. "WE SCORN TO BELIEVE THAT WOMEN ARE UNABLE TO FOCUS, SEE STRAIGHT, OR CARRY 8X10 OUTFITS WITHOUT THE AID OF MASCULINE STRENGTH," WROTE MYRA ALBERT IN THE MARCH, 1894 ISSUE OF THE MAGAZINE. "WE KNOW THEY ARE WILLING TO STAIN THEIR FINGERS WITH PYRO, TO RUIN THEIR COMPLEXIONS IN THE SUNSHINE."

A FEW YEARS EARLIER, CATHERINE WEED BARNES, QUOTED IN THE *PHOTOGRAPHIC TIMES* AND *AMERICAN PHOTOGRAPHER* OF MARCH, 1887, URGED WOMEN TO CONSIDER PHOTOGRAPHY AS A PROFESSION. "A WOMAN MUST LEARN TO IGNORE THE QUESTION OF PERSONAL DAINTINESS. CHEMICALS WILL STAIN, GLASS WILL CUT, AND RUBBER GLOVES ARE A NUISANCE ONLY TO BE ENDURED WHEN THE SOLUTIONS ARE POSITIVELY DANGEROUS."

IN TRADE MAGAZINES LIKE *THE PHOTO-AMERICAN*, *CAMERA CRAFT*, *WILSON'S PHOTOGRAPHIC MAGAZINE* AND *THE PROFESSIONAL PHOTOGRAPHER*, AND IN POPULAR MAGAZINES SUCH AS *ATLANTIC MONTHLY*, *GODEY'S MAGAZINE* AND *THE LADIES' HOME JOURNAL*, ARTICLES WRITTEN BY WOMEN FOR WOMEN PROMOTED THE ART AND CRAFT OF PHOTOGRAPHY. THEY OFFERED HINTS ON CREATING INTERESTING PICTURES AND PORTRAITS, WORKING WITH LIGHTING, MAKING SUPPLIES AT HOME AND USING A DARKROOM.

Mrs. S. Francis Clarke, in a *Photo-American* article from February, 1894, said necessary items for portrait work in the home included "a couple of plain backgrounds, a pair of curtains [and] any chair or other piece of furniture the picture may suggest or the house provide." She advised that "before starting a picture, know exactly what you desire the end to be. Do not start until you have discovered the mood or expression best suited to the desired end." Other how-to articles appealed to female creativity, as women were shown how to make such items as embroidered focusing cloths.

Photographic magazines connected women to new products and suppliers, provided information about technical developments, and, of course, pushed specific brands. *Kodakery*, for example, was a publication launched by the Eastman Kodak Company in 1914. Available by subscription through photographic dealers, it dispensed advice and product news and ran pictures taken by amateur photographers. A year's free subscription was given with each new camera sale. It was published through 1932. Lena Underwood is believed to have been a subscriber and ordered chemicals through this publication.

In addition to information, magazines offered inspiration for those pursuing their hobby out of the mainstream, in communities where they were perhaps the only ones taking pictures.

Wrote Viola Watson in a *Camera Craft* article in January of 1912, "My attic contains a trunkful of photographic magazines, and what beautiful pictures they contain. Looking at them I am filled with emulative zeal."

Edna Benedict of West Meredith, a travel buff and an avid reader of *National Geographic*, was no doubt inspired by its photographs of

EXOTIC LOCALES AND THEIR INHABITANTS. WORKING FROM THE EARLY 1920S TO THE '50S, LENA UNDERWOOD'S WORK ALSO SHOWS SIGNS OF BEING HEAVILY INFLUENCED BY MAGAZINE ARTICLES AND ADVERTISEMENTS. MAGAZINES WERE RELATIVELY INEXPENSIVE THEN. AN ADVERTISEMENT IN THE JULY 11, 1936 *ROXBURY TIMES*, FOR EXAMPLE, OFFERED A PACKAGE DEAL—BUY A SET OF MAGAZINES, FOUR TO SIX TITLES IN A GROUP, FOR SUBSCRIPTIONS RANGING FROM $1.80 TO $2.50 PER YEAR PER GROUP. READERS COULD CHOOSE FROM MAGAZINES LIKE *PICTORIAL REVIEW*, *GENTLEWOMAN*, *McCALL'S*, *MOTHER'S HOME LIFE* AND *NEEDLECRAFT*.

MANY OF UNDERWOOD'S PHOTOS REPRODUCED POSES, PROPS AND SCENES PICTURED IN MAGAZINES AS EXAMPLES FOR ASPIRING PHOTOGRAPHERS. HER PHOTO OF SON DAN BLOWING BUBBLES, EYES CROSSED, MAY HAVE BEEN INSPIRED BY A PAINTING OF A BOY BLOWING BUBBLES WHICH BECAME AN ADVERTISEMENT FOR PEAR'S SOAP AROUND THE TURN OF THE CENTURY. OTHER MAGAZINE ILLUSTRATIONS MIGHT HAVE INFLUENCED HER NORMAN ROCKWELL-LIKE PICTURES, LIKE THE ONE OF A GROUP OF BOYS, ONE WITH HIS FINGERS IN HIS EARS, ABOUT TO LIGHT A FIRE CRACKER.

LENA UNDERWOOD USED A PLAIN BLACK BOX CAMERA TO TAKE THOSE PICTURES, BUT IN THE LATE 1920S, EASTMAN KODAK, AGAIN APPEALING TO FEMALE CONSUMERS, BROUGHT OUT A LINE OF VEST POCKET CAMERAS IN FIVE COLORS—BLUEBIRD (DEEP BLUE), COCKATOO (GREEN), JENNY WREN (BROWN), REDBREAST (RED) AND SEA GULL (GRAY). THE CAMERA, WHICH CAME IN A MATCHING, SILK-LINED CASE, COULD BE PURCHASED WITH THE VANITY ENSEMBLE—A MATCHING LIPSTICK HOLDER, COMPACT, MIRROR, AND CHANGE POCKET. THE ANSCO PHOTOGRAPHIC COMPANY ALSO INTRODUCED A VANITY CAMERA LINE IN 1928. THE COLORED CAMERAS WERE NOT ALTOGETHER SUCCESSFUL, HOWEVER, AS TASTES CHANGED AND THE LESS POPULAR SHADES

WERE LEFT ON DEALERS' SHELVES. BY 1934, MOST CAMERAS WERE AGAIN PRODUCED IN BASIC BLACK.

* * *

WHATEVER THE GIMMICKS USED TO ENTICE THEM TO PHOTOGRAPHY, OR THE METHODS EMPLOYED TO KEEP THEM INTERESTED, WOMEN LIKE ANNA CARROLL, EDNA BENEDICT AND LENA UNDERWOOD USED THEIR CAMERAS IN SOME WAYS TO DEFINE THEIR LIVES. IN PHOTOGRAPHING THEIR NEIGHBORS AND ENVIRONS, THEY BECAME IDENTIFIED AS THE REGISTRARS OF THEIR COMMUNITIES, AND THUS SHAPED THEIR OWN COURSE AS THEY LEFT US A RECORD OF THEIR TIMES.

THEIR PHOTOGRAPHS ARE WINDOWS INTO LONG-AGO LIVES, AND INTO THE HEARTS AND MINDS OF THE WOMEN BEHIND THE CAMERAS. AS PHOTOGRAPHER GERTRUDE KASEBIER SO ELOQUENTLY EXPLAINED, "I HAVE LONGED UNCEASINGLY TO MAKE PICTURES OF PEOPLE, NOT MAPS OF FACES, BUT OF REAL MEN AND WOMEN AS THEY KNOW THEMSELVES, TO MAKE LIKENESSES THAT ARE BIOGRAPHIES, TO BRING OUT IN EACH PHOTOGRAPH THE ESSENTIAL PERSONALITY THAT IS VARIOUSLY CALLED TEMPERAMENT, SOUL, HUMANITY."

GLASS PLATE PHOTOGRAPHY

EDNA GEORGIA BENEDICT AND ANNA CARROLL USED GLASS PLATE CAMERAS TO TAKE MOST OF THEIR PHOTOGRAPHS.

"THE FIRST REQUISITE FOR MAKING GOOD PHOTOGRAPHS IS A GOOD CAMERA," ASSERTED W. I. LINCOLN ADAMS IN HIS 1899 BOOK, *AMATEUR PHOTOGRAPHY*. "THE BEST CAMERA FOR GENERAL USE IS ONE WHICH WILL MAKE PHOTOGRAPHS FOUR BY FIVE INCHES OR FIVE BY EIGHT INCHES, ADJUSTED FOR USE ON A TRIPOD, AND WHICH IS OF A PLAIN PATTERN AND STRONG IN CONSTRUCTION. CAMERAS ARE VERY CHEAP NOW, RANGING IN PRICE FROM TWO DOLLARS AND A HALF TO TWENTY-FIVE DOLLARS. A COMPLETE PHOTOGRAPHIC OUTFIT, INCLUDING A LANDSCAPE LENS, DRY PLATES, DEVELOPING AND PRINTING MATERIALS, MAY BE BOUGHT FOR ONLY TWO DOLLARS AND A HALF. A TRIPOD DOES NOT COST VERY MUCH, THE VERY BEST BEING PRICED AT THREE DOLLARS AND A HALF."

TAKING A PHOTO INVOLVED SCREWING THE CAMERA ONTO THE TRIPOD, AFFIXING THE LENS TO THE CAMERA, THEN FRAMING AND FOCUSING THE SCENE ON THE GROUND GLASS FROM BENEATH A BLACK DRAPE. WHEN THE UPSIDE-DOWN IMAGE SATISFIED THE PHOTOGRAPHER, THE LENS COVER WOULD BE PUT BACK ON, AND THE GROUND GLASS WOULD BE REPLACED WITH A DOUBLE-SIDED PLATE HOLDER CONTAINING TWO LIGHT-SENSITIVE GELATIN DRY GLASS PLATES.

THE FOCUSING CLOTH WOULD BE PLACED OVER THE CAMERA TO EXCLUDE LIGHT LEAKS, AND THE PLATE COVER REMOVED FROM THE GLASS NEGATIVE. THEN THE LENS COVER WOULD BE REMOVED CAREFULLY, TO AVOID JARRING THE CAMERA, AND THE PHOTOGRAPHER WOULD COUNT OFF THE APPROPRIATE NUMBER OF SECONDS FOR THE EXPOSURE, REPLACE THE LENS COVER AND THE PLATE COVER, AND TURNING OVER THE NEGATIVE HOLDER TO TAKE ANOTHER PICTURE.

IN THE CASE OF FLASH PICTURES, A BURNING CANDLE PLACED NEXT TO THE SUBJECT WAS RECOMMENDED FOR USE AS A FOCUSING AID, AND

AFTER ITS REMOVAL FROM THE FRAME, THE PHOTOGRAPHER WOULD REMOVE THE LENS CAP AND TRIGGER A MAGNESIUM CARTRIDGE OR LAMP TO PROVIDE "A LIGHTNING-LIKE FLASH OF THE MOST INTENSE BLUE LIGHT, FOR PERHAPS A THIRTIETH OF A SECOND."

EXPOSED PLATES WERE THEN TAKEN TO A SPECIALLY MADE DARKROOM, OR A CLOSET OR BATHROOM SEALED AGAINST LIGHT LEAKS, AND ILLUMINATED BY A "SAFE" OR RED LIGHT, ALSO CALLED A RUBY LANTERN, WHICH COULD BE PURCHASED FOR BETWEEN FIFTY CENTS AND A DOLLAR AND A QUARTER. THE PLATES WERE SOAKED IN WATER, THEN IMMERSED IN DEVELOPER, WHICH COULD EITHER BE PURCHASED PREPARED OR MADE FROM PYROGALLOL, SULPHITE OF SODA, SULPHUROUS ACID, CARBONATES OF POTASH AND SODA AND WATER. THE NEGATIVES WERE WASHED TWO OR THREE TIMES, AND PLACED IN A FIXING BATH OR HYPOSULFITE OF SODA ("HYPO"). WASHED A FEW MORE TIMES, THE NEGATIVES WERE THEN "HARDENED" IN A SOLUTION OF ALUM AND WATER, WASHED, AND DRIED.

THE DEVELOPED NEGATIVES WERE LATER SECURED IN A WOODEN PRINTING FRAME WITH A SHEET OF PRINT PAPER. IN THE CASE OF SILVER ALBUMIN PRINTING, THE FRAME WAS THEN EXPOSED TO SUNLIGHT FOR A MINUTE OR MORE (THIS BEING THE PRE-ELECTRICITY AGE), AND THE PROCESS REPEATED ACCORDING TO HOW MANY PRINTS WERE DESIRED. THOSE PRINTS WERE THEN PUT IN A TRAY OF WATER TO SOAK BEFORE BEING PLACED IN A TONING BATH (CHLORIDE OF GOLD AND SODIUM BICARBONATE AND ACETATE OF SODA, AND WATER), WHERE THEY REACHED A PURPLISH BROWN COLOR. THEN THEY WERE RINSED AND PLACED IN A FIXING BATH (HYPO, CARBONATE OF SODA, TABLE SALT AND WATER) FOR 15 MINUTES BEFORE BEING WASHED FOR SEVERAL HOURS. AFTER LINE DRYING, THE PRINTS WERE READY FOR MOUNTING.

VELOX PAPER, INTRODUCED IN THE 1890S, CAME IN SEVERAL GRADES AND PROVIDED A VARIETY OF CONTRASTS AND SURFACE TYPES. PRINTS MADE WITH VELOX PAPER, WHICH WAS USED BY BOTH ANNA CARROLL AND EDNA BENEDICT, COULD BE MADE BY PLACING THE PRINTING FRAME IN DIFFUSED SUNLIGHT, A FEW FEET FROM A WINDOW, FOR EXAMPLE, OR THREE OR FOUR INCHES FROM A GAS OR KEROSENE LAMP. VELOX PRINTS WERE DEVELOPED USING SPECIAL DEVELOPING AND FIXING FORMULAS.

CHAPTER 4

THEIR LIVES REMEMBERED:

LENA UNDERWOOD

50 YEARS AFTER IT WAS TAKEN, *LIFE MAGAZINE* PUBLISHED THIS PHOTO OF DAN

MILKING ONE OF UNCLE ANDREW'S COWS.

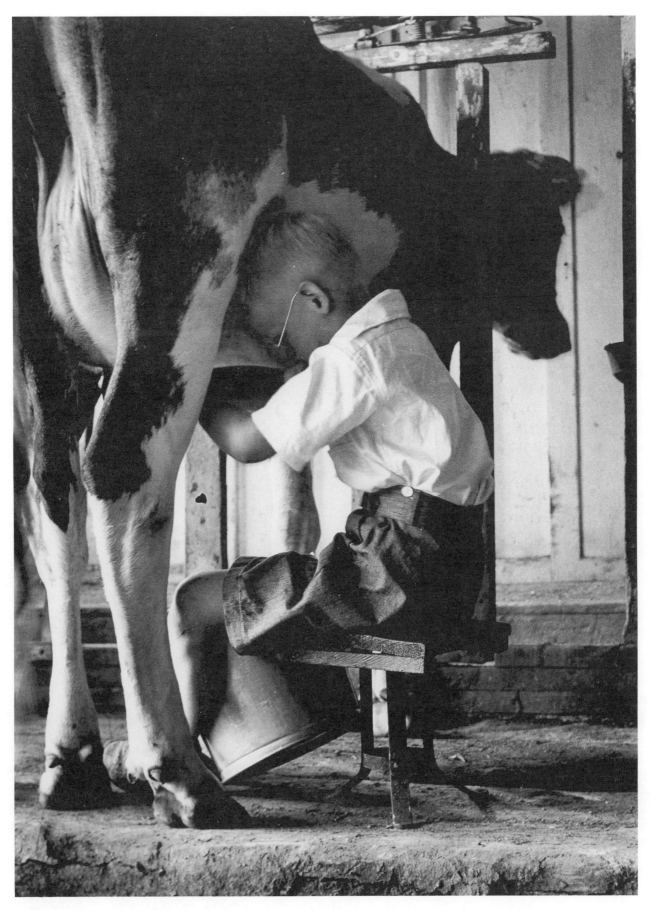

UNDERWOOD CHOSE AN UNUSUAL ANGLE FROM WHICH TO TAKE THIS TIMELESS

PHOTO OF DAN ASLEEP IN HIS PORCH SWING.

For this photo of son Dan blowing bubbles, Underwood may have been inspired by a Pear's Soap advertisement. She also produced a hand-tinted version of this picture.

"YOU'RE NOT SUPPOSED TO SMILE WHEN YOU'VE GOT THE MUMPS," SAID KEN OF

THIS 1938 PHOTO OF HIS BROTHER DAN. BUT UNDERWOOD'S PORTRAITS TENDED

TO SHOW THEIR BOYS AT THEIR BEST.

INFORMAL PORTRAITURE WAS UNDERWOOD'S SPECIALTY, AND THIS SHOT OF

HUSBAND GEORGE AND SON KEN IS A GOOD EXAMPLE.

DAN AND HIS FATHER GEORGE TUNE IN TO THE RADIO.

DAN AND HIS GREAT-AUNT, PHOEBE, READING *MICKEY MOUSE*, DEPICT

UNDERWOOD'S VISION OF SHARING BETWEEN THE GENERATIONS.

A CLASSIC PORTRAIT OF DAN AND KEN.

DAN AND KEN POSED IN THEIR ONE-PIECE BATHING SUITS WHILE SWIMMING AT

STRATTON FALLS.

Dan and Ken were shown reading on the sofa beneath another portrait of the brothers and Underwood's hand-tinted photo of a cherry tree.

Underwood earned additional income for the family by producing Christmas cards from photos such as this one of May Stewart's fireplace, with stockings hung from the mantle.

THE CONTRAST OF WHITE SWAN AND DARK WATER MAKES THIS A STRIKING PHOTO.

IT WAS TAKEN IN KIRKSIDE PARK.

This portrait of Lena Underwood, believed taken in the late 1920s, shows the photographer with a snapshot album.

THIS SHOT OF THE BOYS READING ON THE LAWN IS ANOTHER EXAMPLE OF

UNDERWOOD'S INTEREST IN POSING SUBJECTS IN INFORMAL SETTINGS.

Children were a favorite subject of Underwood's. Here, Dan, Ken and

two of the McCaffre neighbors work in the garden.

CHILDREN ENJOYING LOLLIPOPS REFLECT UNDERWOOD'S BELIEF THAT

YOUNGSTERS SHOULD WORK, TIDY UP AND BE REWARDED.

HER FIRST FLASH PHOTO SHOWS UNDERWOOD'S SON KEN, PERCHED ON A CATALOG

DOING SCHOOLWORK .

Underwood's brother Charlie Bouton, right, posed with hired man Charlie Dart and a boy believed to be Dart's son, on the Bouton farm in West Settlement, Roxbury, circa 1922. It is unlike many of Underwood's photographs, which usually focus on the domestic side of life.

Christmas dinner in the late 1930's was captured in this photo of family and friends gathered around the holiday table. (L. to R.) Ken, Dan, neighbor Tom Cantwell, friend Merrit Curran and Andrew and Ethel Underwood.

UNDERWOOD WAS ALSO AN ACCOMPLISHED LANDSCAPE PHOTOGRAPHER. THIS

SNOW SCENE WAS TAKEN AT KIRKSIDE PARK IN ROXBURY AND WAS AMONG THOSE

THE PHOTOGRAPHER CHOSE TO HAND TINT.

Lena Bouton Underwood

When Lena Bouton Underwood died in 1990 at the age of 100, she had witnessed half of Roxbury's history—the rise and fall of the area's farm economy, the hey-day of the railroad and accompanying tourist trade, the Great Depression, two world wars, and decades of relative peace and plenty.

Through many of those years of boom and bust, sacrifice and prosperity, Lena Underwood carried a camera. Between the 1920s and 1950s, much of what went on in her home and community was framed by the viewfinder as she shaped the images that would survive her.

Born February 3, 1890, Lena was the daughter of George and Elvira Mead Bouton, a member of one of the town's pioneering families. She and brother Charles grew up on the West Settlement farm where railroad tycoon and financier Jay Gould had been born in 1856. Gould had risen from humble rural beginnings to a position of great wealth and power, and his family's influence on Roxbury would reverberate throughout Lena's life.

George Bouton, Underwood's father, bought the famous homestead from the Gould estate, and Lena helped her brother run it after their parents' deaths until, at the age of 36, she married George Underwood on March 26, 1926. He, too, was descended from one of Roxbury's earliest families. The son of Daniel T. and Eliza Coonley Underwood, and the grandson of prominent physician Dr. Oliver Underwood, George was born May 13, 1889. A World War I veteran, he

SERVED IN FRANCE IN COMPANY B OF THE 59TH PIONEERS, AND RETURNED TO HELP HIS BROTHER ANDREW RUN THE FAMILY FARM ON STRATTON FALLS ROAD NEXT TO THE OLD SCHOOL BAPTIST "YELLOW" CHURCH.

WHEN GEORGE AND ANDREW DECIDED TO END THEIR FARM PARTNERSHIP, GEORGE GOT A JOB AS CARETAKER OF AN ESTATE IN GLEN COVE, LONG ISLAND. HE AND HIS WIFE SPENT ABOUT A YEAR THERE, UNTIL THEIR FIRST SON WAS BORN IN 1927. SINCE ESTATE EMPLOYEES WERE NOT ALLOWED TO HAVE CHILDREN WITH THEM, THE UNDERWOODS RETURNED TO ROXBURY, WHERE THEY MOVED IN WITH UNDERWOOD'S AGED AUNT, PHOEBE MEAD, ON LAKE STREET IN THE VILLAGE. GEORGE WORKED AS A CARPENTER BEFORE HE WAS HIRED BY FINLEY SHEPARD, HUSBAND OF JAY GOULD'S DAUGHTER, HELEN.

THE SHEPARDS WERE SUMMER RESIDENTS OF KIRKSIDE, THE ELEGANT VILLAGE HOME HELEN HAD ESTABLISHED NEXT TO THE STONE CHURCH SHE AND HER SIBLINGS HAD CONSTRUCTED IN HER FATHER'S MEMORY AFTER HIS DEATH IN 1892. HELEN AND FINLEY MAINTAINED A LARGE ESTATE WHICH GREW TO INCLUDE GUEST HOUSES, A PARK, LAKE, GOLF COURSE, TENNIS COURTS AND A GREENHOUSE. MANY LOCAL PEOPLE, INCLUDING CARPENTER GEORGE UNDERWOOD WHO WORKED UNDER SUPERINTENDENT S. G. LUTZ, WERE EMPLOYED TO KEEP THE ESTATE IN ORDER. THE COMMUNITY ALSO BENEFITTED BY THE PHILANTHROPY OF HELEN GOULD, WHO BUILT A YMCA AND LIBRARY IN TOWN.

GEORGE AND LENA UNDERWOOD CARED FOR HER AUNT PHOEBE UNTIL SHE PASSED AWAY AT THE AGE OF 92. ALONG WITH THE UNDERWOOD BOYS, DAN AND KEN, THE HOUSEHOLD INCLUDED UNDERWOOD'S BROTHER AND SISTER-IN-LAW, CHARLES AND TILLIE STICKLES BOUTON, WHO LOST THE WEST SETTLEMENT FARM IN THE DEPRESSION. THEY HAD NO CHILDREN, AND MADE THEIR HOME WITH THE UNDERWOODS UNTIL CHARLES DIED IN 1957, AND HIS WIFE WAS LATER PLACED IN A NURSING HOME.

Somehow, with all the work required in this extended family—gardening, cooking, cleaning, mending—Lena Underwood managed to develop a busy photography business. It had started out as a hobby, with Lena influenced by a close friend, Lena Corbin, a school teacher who was also an amateur photographer. (Ironically, Lena Corbin grew up in Meeker Hollow, near the farm where another subject of this book, Anna Carroll, spent her childhood.) Together, the two Lenas would practice their craft by taking pictures of friends and relatives in Roxbury. Lena Corbin became a teacher in Amsterdam, N.Y. Eventually Lena Underwood's skill and interest in photography developed beyond a recreational pursuit.

Underwood started as a rural professional in the early 1930s, when Maurice Fanning, an optometrist who owned a jewelry and stationery store in Roxbury from 1908 to 1945, encouraged her to process rolls of film brought to his store by summer visitors. Mr. Fanning, long-time Roxbury postmaster and founder and manager of the Roxbury Theater, also dabbled in photography. An account of the wedding of Virginia Haight and Harold Finch in the April 27, 1935 *Roxbury Times* stated that he took pictures of the wedding party, and he is known to have distributed postcards of the community bearing photos he had taken.

But Lena Underwood is remembered as the community's primary chronicler. Along with her photos of family and community activities, she took license photos, wedding pictures, baby and family portraits, even funeral photographs, all without advertising. While by today's standards her prices were minimal (one fee, which she scribbled on the back of an envelope, showed she charged a customer 60 cents for film,

15 CENTS FOR DEVELOPING AND $1.26 FOR 18 PRINTS), THE MONEY SHE EARNED FOR THIS WORK SUPPLIED BETWEEN A QUARTER AND A THIRD OF THE FAMILY'S INCOME DURING THE LEAN 1930S, ACCORDING TO SON DAN.

ALTHOUGH SHE WAS A SINGLE, STRONG-WILLED YOUNG WOMAN WHEN THE WOMEN'S SUFFRAGE DEBATES WERE GOING ON IN ROXBURY BETWEEN 1916 AND 1919, LENA UNDERWOOD WAS MORE INTERESTED IN SUPPLEMENTING THE FAMILY'S INCOME WITH HER PHOTOGRAPHY THAN IN USING IT TO DECLARE HER INDEPENDENCE. AND FAR FROM FEELING THREATENED BY HIS WIFE'S PROFESSIONAL ACTIVITY, GEORGE UNDERWOOD RECOGNIZED ITS WORTH, SAYS THEIR SON DAN. "HE WAS VERY SUPPORTIVE. SHE [MOTHER] DIDN'T DRIVE, SO HE WOULD TAKE HER WHERE SHE HAD TO GO, MOVE THE PROPS, HOLD THE LIGHTS." THIS CONTINUED AFTER GEORGE UNDERWOOD LOST HIS JOB WHEN THE SHEPARD ESTATE WAS CLOSED UPON THE DEATH OF FINLEY SHEPARD IN 1942 (HELEN GOULD SHEPARD HAD DIED IN 1938).

UNDERWOOD'S SONS, TOO, WOULD LEND A HAND WHEN NEEDED. "WHEN I GOT OLD ENOUGH, I'D GO WITH HER TO SHOOT PHOTOGRAPHS," SAYS DAN, WHO AT ONE TIME MADE A TRIPOD FOR HIS MOTHER. "BUT ONE THING I DIDN'T LIKE WAS TO GO TAKE FUNERAL PHOTOS."

SOME OF DAN'S EARLIEST MEMORIES INCLUDE PEOPLE COMING INTO THE UNDERWOOD HOME TO HAVE LICENSE PHOTOS AND OTHER PORTRAITS TAKEN. "WE HAD THIS BIG WINDOW. MOM WOULD PULL DOWN THE SHADE FOR A BACKDROP. SHE HAD A BIG FLOOD LIGHT SINCE THERE WASN'T ANY FLASH BACK THEN." CUSTOMERS WOULD ALSO BRING IN PHOTOS THEY WANTED COPIED. SHE USED A HOME-MADE COPY STAND, AND A LARGE CAMERA WITH A PORTRAIT LENS, THAT EMPLOYED A FILM PACK, RATHER THAN ROLL FILM.

UNDERWOOD'S DARKROOM WAS LOCATED OFF THE LIVING ROOM AND HAD ORIGINALLY BEEN BUILT AS A PANTRY. SONS DAN AND KEN CONTRIBUTED THE

FOLLOWING DESCRIPTION:

IT WAS LIKE A LITTLE CLOSET ABOUT 6X6. THERE WAS A CUPBOARD IN THERE AND A DOOR WHICH WENT DOWN INTO THE CELLAR. SHE CLOSED IT OFF WITH A BENCH AND HAD THE ENLARGER SITTING THERE. SHE DID SOME EXPERIMENTS IN ENLARGING AND SUPERIMPOSING OF IMAGES. BUT IT WAS A VERY BASIC DARKROOM.

TO BEGIN, SHE'D CARRY THE WATER IN FROM THE KITCHEN AND MIX UP THE STUFF. THE DEVELOPER SHE'D MIX UP BEFOREHAND AND KEEP IT IN THERE IN THE DARK. THERE WOULD BE PEOPLE WHO WANTED THEIR PICTURES RIGHT AWAY, SO SHE'D GO IN THE DARKROOM IN TOTAL DARKNESS AND OPEN UP THE CAMERA, PULL OUT THE FILM AND DEVELOP IT.

[WHEN MAKING PRINTS,] SHE'D PUT THE PRINT IN A TRAY, THEN ROCK IT BACK AND FORTH, GOING FROM DEVELOPER, TO WATER TO HYPO THEN WATER TO WASH IT. SHE'D STICK THEM ON BOARDS OUTSIDE AND LET THE SUN DRY THEM. WHEN THEY FELL OFF, THEY WERE DRY. FOR TINTED PICTURES, SHE USED MATTE, NOT GLOSSY PAPER. SHE ALSO HAD A GADGET FOR EMBOSSING THE MATS AROUND THE PHOTOGRAPHS. IT WAS A BOARD WITH A ROLLER. SHE'D PUT A PICTURE ON THE BOARD IN THE GROOVE AND ROLL THE ROLLER OVER IT TO EMBOSS IT.

UNDERWOOD OCCASIONALLY OPENED HER DARKROOM TO INTERESTED STUDENTS. WALTER MEADE OF ROXBURY, WHO WAS TO BECOME AN ACCOMPLISHED NATURE PHOTOGRAPHER SPECIALIZING IN CATSKILL WILDLIFE, REPORTEDLY RECEIVED A LESSON OR TWO FROM UNDERWOOD, AS DID THE MEMBERS OF A PHOTOGRAPHY CLUB FROM THE LOCAL SCHOOL. "MRS. NELSON CAME OVER WITH A CLASS FROM SCHOOL TO LEARN HOW TO DEVELOP," UNDERWOOD WROTE IN HER DIARY ON MARCH 8, 1954.

IN THE MID-TO-LATE 1930S, UNDERWOOD, WHO WAS ALSO INTERESTED IN LANDSCAPE SKETCHING AND DRAWING, COMBINED HER SKILLS AS A PHOTOGRAPHER WITH HER ARTISTIC LEANINGS AND BEGAN HAND-TINTING PHOTOGRAPHS. USING

COTTON-TIPPED TOOTHPICKS DAUBED IN OIL PAINTS, SHE PAINSTAKINGLY ADDED COLOR TO BLACK-AND-WHITE PRINTS BEFORE THE ADVENT OF COLOR FILM.

AN EXAMPLE OF THE TYPE OF JOBS SHE DID CAN BE FOUND IN AN UNDATED LETTER FROM AN ONEONTA CUSTOMER: "I AM ENCLOSING TWO FILMS. COLOR THEM IN ABOUT A FIFTY-CENT SIZE (EACH) . . .THE ONE IS OF MILDRED'S TWO CHILDREN IN A BED OF ALL COLORS OF TULIPS (IN NEAWAH PARK). THE OTHER IS MADELINE IN HER BIRTHDAY DRESS OF YELLOW AND THE ROSES BACK OF HER WERE SHADED PINK. OUR HOUSE IS BROWN, TRIMMED IN WHITE, BUT I AM NOT PARTICULAR ABOUT THOSE COLORS, ONLY HER YELLOW OUTFIT. I AM NOT IN ANY RUSH, ONLY TO HAVE THE ONE OF THE BABIES FOR AN EASTER GIFT FOR MILDRED."

NETTIE FAWCETT OF JOHNSON CITY SENT A SIMILAR REQUEST: "I HAVE A NEGATIVE OF LEE THAT I WOULD LIKE VERY MUCH TO HAVE ENLARGED. I WOULD LIKE FIVE. . . I WOULD LIKE THEM IN COLORS IF YOU CAN. THE GIRLS WANT TO GIVE IT TO THEIR DAD. THE SUIT IS [SIC] KAKI COLOR, A LITTLE DARKER THAN THE SUMMER SUITS. THE SHOES ARE DARK BROWN. THE BELT IS EITHER DARK BROWN OR BLACK. . . DOES HE EVER LOOK SWELL. THIS NEGATIVE WAS TAKEN IN LOUISIANA. RIGHT NOW HE IS IN CALIFORNIA, IN THE DESERT."

UNDERWOOD BECAME NOTED FOR HER ARTISTRY, AND WAS MUCH IN DEMAND DURING THE CHRISTMAS SEASON, WHEN SHE MADE PERSONALIZED CARDS FOR CUSTOMERS. SHE ORDERED A CHRISTMAS CARD PRODUCTION KIT FROM GEORGE MURPHY, INC. OF NEW YORK CITY. A NEGATIVE OF A PHOTOGRAPH, SUCH AS A HEARTH WITH STOCKINGS HUNG ON THE MANTLE AND CAT CURLED BEFORE THE FIREPLACE, WOULD BE PUT IN THE OPENING OF A PRE-CUT MASK AND A PRINT TAKEN OF IT. THE BLACK AND WHITE IMAGE WAS OFTENTIMES COLORED, AND A GREETING WAS ADDED.

AMONG HER CUSTOMERS WERE MEMBERS OF THE GOULD FAMILY. HELEN GOULD SNOW, WHOSE MOTHER ALICE SNOW WROTE A BIOGRAPHY OF HER FAMOUS

COUSIN HELEN GOULD SHEPARD, WAS A SEASONAL RESIDENT OF ROXBURY. WRITING FROM HER WINTER HOME IN YONKERS IN 1937, MRS. SNOW SAID, "THE PICTURE FOR MRS. SHEPARD HAS BEEN RECEIVED AND WE ALL THINK IT IS BEAUTIFUL. IT WILL BE FRAMED IN TIME FOR CHRISTMAS."

MRS. SNOW RAISED PERSIAN CATS AND GAVE A FELINE NAMED GINGER TO THE UNDERWOODS. DAN RECALLS BEING SENT OUT TO PICK CATNIP LEAVES SO MRS. SNOW COULD DRY THEM FOR HER PETS. THE CATS WERE NOT ONLY PAMPERED, BUT PHOTOGRAPHED AS WELL. IN 1939, HELEN SNOW SENT UNDERWOOD A REQUEST FROM YONKERS. "I AM SENDING MY FOLDER OF PUFF TO BE COLORED. EVERY ONE ELSE IS FRAMING THEIRS, SO I WANT ONE TO FRAME."

ONE OF UNDERWOOD'S MOST DIFFICULT JOBS INVOLVED THE GOULD CHURCH AND ITS SPECTACULAR TIFFANY STAINED GLASS WINDOWS. "ONE MAN CAME TO HER AND WANTED HER TO TAKE PHOTOS OF THE WINDOWS AND TINT THEM," RECALLED SON KEN. "IT WAS QUITE A JOB. SHE TOOK THE PHOTOS AND THEN SAT WAY UP ON TOP OF THIS 12-FOOT STEP LADDER FOR ABOUT A WEEK AND COLORED THE PHOTOGRAPHS, GETTING THE COLOR RIGHT. SHE GOT ABOUT A DOLLAR FOR THEM."

KEN ALSO RECALLS THAT HIS MOTHER OCCASIONALLY TOOK SOME ARTISTIC LICENSE WITH HER HAND-TINTED PHOTOS. "SHE LIKED TO PUT SUNSETS IN PICTURES," HE SAID. "NO MATTER IF THE PHOTO HAD BEEN TAKEN IN THE NORTH OR EAST, SHE'D PUT A SUNSET IN." SNOW, TOO, WAS A PASSION OF UNDERWOOD'S. "IF THERE WAS A BIG SNOWSTORM, SHE'D LOOK OUTSIDE AND SAY, 'OH, WE HAVE TO GO OUT AND TAKE PICTURES'," KEN RELATED.

UNDERWOOD AND HER CAMERA WERE A FAMILIAR SIGHT AROUND ROXBURY, AS SHE PHOTOGRAPHED SPECIAL EVENTS, GROUPS, LANDMARKS AND BUILDINGS. AND IN THE 1930S AND '40S, ROXBURY WAS A BUSY PLACE, WITH MORE THAN 2,260 PEOPLE IN THE TOWNSHIP. SCANNING THE ROXBURY TIMES FOR THE YEAR

1934, MEETINGS AND ACTIVITIES HELD BY NO LESS THAN 15 CIVIC AND CHURCH GROUPS CAN BE FOUND. ORGANIZATIONS MENTIONED INCLUDED THE READING CLUB, THE ODD FELLOWS AND THEIR WOMEN'S AFFILIATE, THE REBEKAHS, THE ROXBURY MEN'S CLUB, THE LADIES SOCIAL SOCIETY AND MISSIONARY AUXILIARY OF THE JAY GOULD MEMORIAL REFORMED CHURCH, THE MASONS AND THEIR FEMALE COUNTERPARTS IN THE ORDER OF THE EASTERN STAR, THE EPWORTH LEAGUE AND LADIES AID SOCIETY OF THE METHODIST CHURCH (OF WHICH UNDERWOOD WAS A MEMBER), THE BOY AND GIRL SCOUTS, THE ROXBURY FISH & GAME CLUB, THE 4-H CLUB, THE FIRE DEPARTMENT, A TOWN BAND, SUMMER BASEBALL TEAM AND THE PTA.

WHILE HER BOYS WERE IN SCHOOL, LENA WAS A MEMBER OF THE PTA. AT THE OCTOBER 23, 1935 MEETING OF THE GROUP, WHEN MISS EDNA LAWRENCE OF ONEONTA HIGH SCHOOL ATTEMPTED TO ANSWER THE QUESTION, "WHAT VOCATION SHALL I CHOOSE FOR MY CHILD?," UNDERWOOD WAS ON THE REFRESHMENT COMMITTEE.

MANY OF HER PHOTOGRAPHS FOCUSED ON SCHOOL AND THE ACTIVITIES IN WHICH DAN AND KEN WERE INVOLVED. "SHE TOOK A PHOTO WHEN WE PUT ON *TOM SAWYER*," RECALLED KEN. "SHE PROBABLY USED A MAGNESIUM BULB. SHE HAD TO CHANGE BULBS AFTER EVERY PICTURE."

FROM THE TIME THEY WERE BABIES, THE UNDERWOOD BOYS TOLERATED MUCH POSING, PRIMPING AND PICTURE TAKING. SAYS KEN, "I CAN REMEMBER BEING CHASED IN AND GOTTEN DRESSED AND SHOVED OUT AND POSED. IT SEEMED LIKE ABOUT EVERY OTHER DAY. IT WAS PROBABLY A BIGGER STRUGGLE TO GET US WASHED AND DRESSED FOR THE PICTURES THAN TO ACTUALLY TAKE THE PHOTOS."

HE REMEMBERED ONE INSTANCE WHEN HIS MOTHER PHOTOGRAPHED BROTHER DAN, WHO WAS SUFFERING FROM THE MUMPS. "SHE TIED THE KERCHIEF AROUND HIM AND PUT A TIE ON HIM TO TAKE THE PHOTO. AND HE'S SMILING. . .

YOU'RE NOT SUPPOSED TO SMILE WHEN YOU'VE GOT THE MUMPS."

IN MANY OF HER PHOTOGRAPHS, UNDERWOOD DEPICTS ONE OR BOTH BOYS DOING DOMESTIC CHORES, SUCH AS SEWING, LETTER WRITING AND GARDENING. SHE LOOKED FOR BACKGROUNDS AND STAGED SITUATIONS TO BRING OUT THE BEST IN HER CHILDREN AND IN HER PHOTOGRAPHY. SHE POSSESSED A SPECIAL EYE FOR DETAIL AND STORYTELLING IN HER PHOTOS. IN A SERIES OF DAN, KEN AND NEIGHBORHOOD CHILDREN RAKING LEAVES, CLEANING UP AND SUCKING LOLLIPOPS, SHE ALSO PROVIDES HER VIEW OF A PROPER CHILD'S ROUTINE, AND MAKES A STATEMENT TO ALL MOTHERS: CHILDREN SHOULD WORK, TIDY UP AND THEN RECEIVE A TREAT.

HER USE OF PROPS AND HOUSEHOLD FEATURES ALSO WORKED TO CONVEY THE DESIRED IMAGE. KEN AND HIS FATHER BY THE RADIO SHOWED THE FAMILY WITH THIS TECHNOLOGICAL BREAK-THROUGH; DAN READING WITH HIS GREAT-AUNT PHOEBE DEPICTED THE CONNECTION BETWEEN YOUNG AND OLD. AUNT PHOEBE IS REMEMBERED FOR HER DAILY BIBLE READINGS AND HER METHODICAL WAYS— "SHE'D TAKE A STICK AND SMOOTH OUT EVERY LAYER OF HER BED," RELATED KEN. UNDERWOOD'S PHOTOGRAPHS OF MANY WOMEN HIGHLIGHTED SUCH MORAL VIRTUES, AS WELL AS THEIR SOCIAL STATUS. IN A SERIES OF FIVE PHOTOGRAPHS, SHE DEPICTED A MRS. WILLIAMS OF ROXBURY AS A WOMAN OF MIDDLE-CLASS LEISURE IN THE MID-1930S. THE SUBJECT IS SHOWN ARRANGING FLOWERS, GAILY SOCIALIZING ON THE TELEPHONE, TENDING A BIRD IN ITS CAGE, READING THE BIBLE AND SITTING AT HER PIANO, ALL RESPECTABLE AND ENVIABLE PASTIMES AND ATTRIBUTES.

BUT NOT ALL OF LENA UNDERWOOD'S PHOTOGRAPHS WERE PLANNED OR STAGED. HER AWARD-WINNING SHOT OF EIGHT-YEAR-OLD DAN PERCHED ON A STOOL WITH A BUCKET BETWEEN HIS KNEES AS HE MILKED ONE OF UNCLE ANDREW'S COWS WAS A SPONTANEOUS ONE. "IT WASN'T A BIG DEAL, SHE JUST

HAPPENED TO BE THERE," DAN RECALLS. SHE WAS EVEN ON HAND FOR AN OCCASIONAL NEWS EVENT, LIKE THE 1924 LOCOMOBILE ACCIDENT OR THE BURNING OF STUB CASWELL'S PAINT STORE, THE FORMER BROWER AND LONG GARAGE, IN 1956.

LENA UNDERWOOD CONTINUED TO RECORD THE COMINGS AND GOINGS OF DAILY LIFE THROUGH THE 1950S WHEN SHE WAS IN HER SIXTIES. DIARY ENTRIES TELL OF WEATHER, WORK, VISITS FROM FRIENDS, FAMILY MILESTONES, AND OF COURSE WHETHER PHOTOS WERE PART OF THEM. ON MOTHER'S DAY, 1953, SHE NOTED THAT "DANNY, BETTY AND DAVIE WERE HERE FOR DINNER. TOOK PICTURES." FRIDAY, JAN. 14, 1955: "TOOK FIRST PICTURES OF JOHNNIE, SIX WEEKS OLD." AND ON AUGUST 19 OF THAT YEAR, SHE NOTED, "WATER VERY HIGH, TOOK PICTURES."

ON JUNE 26, 1955, SHE WROTE THE WORDS OF A PROUD GRANDPARENT: "DAVIE SPOKE HIS FIRST PIECE IN CHURCH—CHILDREN'S DAY TODAY—THREE YEARS, THREE MONTHS OLD." DAVID WOULD LATER FOLLOW HIS GRANDMOTHER AS A CAMERA BUFF, DEVELOPING HIS HOBBY IN THE AIR FORCE AND CARRYING IT INTO WORK AS A NEWSPAPER DARKROOM TECHNICIAN.

GRADUALLY, UNDERWOOD, WHO WAS BOTHERED BY RHEUMATISM AND WAS LEFT A WIDOW BY GEORGE'S PASSING IN 1974, CEASED TO TAKE HER CAMERA EVERYWHERE. "SHE DIDN'T GET WITH THE MODERN CAMERAS," SAYS KEN. HIS BROTHER PLACED THE END OF THEIR MOTHER'S PHOTOGRAPHIC CAREER WHEN COLOR FILM WAS INTRODUCED.

BUT A LIFETIME OF IMAGES HAD BEEN INDELIBLY ETCHED IN HER MEMORY. ONE OF THOSE, A PHOTOGRAPH OF KEN WITH A PET CROW PERCHED ON HIS SHOULDER, HAD ALWAYS BEEN A FAVORITE OF LENA'S. "WHEN SHE WAS 100, THAT'S WHAT SHE COULD REMEMBER," SAID HER SON.

LENA UNDERWOOD DIED JUNE 28, 1990 AT THE DELAWARE COUNTY INFIRMARY IN DELHI.

CHAPTER 5

THEIR LIVES REMEMBERED:

EDNA BENEDICT

ALFRED G. SMITH ON A BICYCLE. THE COLLECTION ALSO INCLUDES A PHOTOGRAPH
OF BENEDICT ON THE SAME BICYCLE, EVIDENTLY TAKEN AT THE SAME TIME, ON HER
BIRTHDAY, JULY 19, 1905.

West Meredith matriarchs, neighbors from Warner Hill Road. Included are Mrs. Smith, Mrs. Georgia, Mrs. Cole and Mrs. Bell. Benedict took this photo on an outing September 6, 1909.

Benedict photographed brother Wendell Georgia and his dog Prince in 1915. Wendell is remembered as the prankster in the family, continually teasing and pulling practical jokes on other family members.

The Georgia homestead's mill pond.

A CLUB FROM THE DELAWARE LITERARY INSTITUTE WAS PHOTOGRAPHED

PICNICKING AT STRADER'S LAKE IN 1908.

THE GEORGIA HOMESTEAD, WITH ITS DAM AND MILLPOND.

A WINTER VIEW OF WARNER HILL, WITH THE GEORGIA MILL AND FARM BUILDINGS

IN FOREGROUND, SHOWS BENEDICT'S INTEREST IN WORKING LANDSCAPES.

IN THIS PORTRAIT OF STUDENTS AT HER FORMER SCHOOL, BENEDICT POSED THE STUDENTS PROUDLY IN FRONT OF THE LOU STRONG SCHOOLHOUSE (LATER TO BE THE HOWARD BENEDICT SCHOOL) IN WEST MEREDITH.

Mary Georgia's Sunday School class from the Treadwell Methodist Church posed for this 1915 photo.

LESLIE BELL ON THE PORCH IN 1910.

Andrew and Mary Georgia and children Wendell and Edna, posed for this 1908 family portrait, which Benedict took by setting up the camera before joining the group.

THE McNEILLY FAMILY, INCLUDING TWO DOGS, WAS GROUPED ON THE FRONT LAWN

OF THEIR WEST MEREDITH HOME.

ALBERT HOWE DRAWING MILK TO THE PINES CREAMERY, THE GEORGIA FARM IN

THE BACKGROUND.

The Pines Creamery, with workers Ed Bell and Clarence Delameter. The coming of the railroad meant farms like the Georgia's and the Benedict's could take their milk to processing plants like this rather than churn most of it into butter.

ANDREW AND WENDELL GEORGIA WITH A LOAD OF HAY.

MELVIN HOWE PROUDLY DISPLAYS HIS HANDSOME TEAM.

THROUGH A WOMAN'S EYE | 117

BENEDICT CAPTURED FATHER ANDREW AND BROTHER WENDELL CUTTING CORN.

THROUGH A WOMAN'S EYE | 119

BENEDICT TOOK THIS SPRINGTIME PHOTO OF THE GEORGIA FARMHOUSE, HER

CHILDHOOD HOME, FROM THE DELHI-TREADWELL ROAD.

EDNA GEORGIA (RIGHT) AND ANNA McNEILLY BOTH TAUGHT AT ONE-ROOM
SCHOOLS IN WEST MEREDITH.

THIS FORMAL PHOTOGRAPH OF BENEDICT MAY BE A SELF-PORTRAIT.

EDNA GEORGIA BENEDICT

ASKED TO DESCRIBE EDNA GEORGIA BENEDICT, FRIENDS AND RELATIVES INVARIABLY SPEAK OF HER GOOD CHEER, HER BOUNDLESS ENERGY, HER DEVOTION TO THE CHURCH—AND HER LOVE OF PHOTOGRAPHY. FOR EDNA BENEDICT WAS ALMOST NEVER WITHOUT A CAMERA, WHETHER TO PHOTOGRAPH BOATERS ON THE MILL POND, COWS IN THE MEADOW OR CHILDREN AT THEIR ONE-ROOM SCHOOL. "PHOTOGRAPHY WAS A GREAT INTEREST OF HERS. SHE OFTEN TOOK HER CAMERA FOR CANDID SNAPSHOTS OF PICNICS, SCENIC DRIVES AND SPECIAL OCCASIONS," RELATES HER NIECE, CHRISTINA JONES.

IT'S NOT CLEAR WHERE SHE DEVELOPED AN INTEREST IN PHOTOGRAPHY. SHE MAY HAVE BEEN INFLUENCED BY MAGAZINE ARTICLES AND ADVERTISEMENTS OF THE TIME, OR BY STUDENTS OR TEACHERS AT THE DELAWARE LITERARY INSTITUTE WHICH SHE ATTENDED. SHE MAY ALSO HAVE BEEN INSPIRED BY AMATEUR OR PROFESSIONAL PHOTOGRAPHERS PASSING THROUGH HER RURAL COMMUNITY OF WEST MEREDITH. THE *DELAWARE DAIRYMAN* OF JULY 5, 1907, FOR INSTANCE, CONTAINED AN ITEM ABOUT HAROLD PARSONS OF BINGHAMTON WHO WAS VACATIONING WITH COUSINS GEORGE AND ALMON PRIME IN WEST MEREDITH. THE PAPER FOUND IT WORTH NOTING THAT MR. PARSONS "HAS HIS CAMERA AND TAKES FINE PICTURES."

EDNA GEORGIA WAS 19 THAT YEAR, A STUDENT AT THE LITERARY INSTITUTE IN FRANKLIN WHERE SHE WAS TRAINING TO BECOME A TEACHER. IT WAS ONE OF THE FEW OCCUPATIONS OPEN TO RURAL WOMEN OF THE TIME, FOR THIS WAS FARM COUNTRY, WHERE LIFE FOR FEMALES REVOLVED AROUND TENDING THE HOME AND GARDEN, AND HELPING THE MEN WITH LIVESTOCK, FIELD WORK AND RELATED CHORES.

Edna was born July 19, 1888 to Andrew Fortner and Mary Stewart Smith Georgia. She had a brother, Wendell, seven years her junior, and grew up on a farm at the juncture of Warner Hill Road and the Delhi-Treadwell Road in the town of Meredith.

Father Andrew Georgia, son of David and Lovina Fortner Georgia who lived nearby, was an enterprising man. In addition to a dairy operation, milk from which was taken to the Meridale Farms Creamery, he ran water-powered saw and grist mills, which were important to their farm neighbors.

"My father would bring home corn meal and buckwheat from the mill," recalled Helen Oliver Prime. "My mother thought Andrew could grind it at his mill better than anyone else. Andrew Georgia's land was kept like a landscape garden, his fences so straight and well-made, and no rubbish to be seen."

Andrew's son Wendell grew up to assist his father with the farm and mills. Stewart Georgia, son of Wendell and Carrie Osterhout Georgia, provides this recollection of the operation: "The pond was small, two to three acres, held back by an earthen dam. At the dam, in the middle, was a saw mill. The saw mill and grist mill shared the water. [There were] two water wheels. One was small and ran smaller machinery, such as the jig saw, the lathe, drill press and the 40-volt hydro-electric plant, [which] supplied the house and perhaps the barn with a limited supply of electricity. The larger water wheel was used for the six-foot grind stones, which ground grain for the neighbors, generally barley, buckwheat and oats. The larger wheel was also used to saw logs. At some times of year, eels would get caught in the big water wheel, at which time someone would have to climb down on to the

WHEEL AND CUT THEM OUT, SO THE WHEEL WOULD TURN FREELY.

CONNECTED TO THE MILL WAS A WORKSHOP FOR WOOD. MY FATHER AND GRANDFATHER WERE BOTH VERY CAPABLE WITH THEIR HANDS AND ENJOYED MAKING THINGS OUT OF WOOD. AN ICE HOUSE WAS ALSO CONNECTED TO THE MILL, AND WAS FILLED WITH ICE FROM THE POND EACH WINTER."

THE DAM WAS WASHED OUT IN A 1935 FLOOD, TWO YEARS BEFORE ANDREW PASSED AWAY AT THE AGE OF 80.

STEWART GEORGIA ALSO RECALLED A SMALL WATER WHEEL IN THE HOUSE, WHERE WATER FROM A HILLSIDE RESERVOIR WAS USED TO PROVIDE POWER TO CHURN CREAM TO MAKE BUTTER. "I ALSO THINK THEY MAY HAVE HAD A WASHING MACHINE CONNECTED TO THIS SAME SOURCE OF POWER," HE RELATED.

BENEDICT GREW UP HELPING HER MOTHER WITH HOUSEHOLD DUTIES AND ASSISTING WITH SOME FARM WORK. SHE AND HER BROTHER ATTENDED A ONE-ROOM SCHOOL ON WARNER HILL ROAD HALF A MILE FROM THEIR HOME. THEIRS WAS A DEVOUT FAMILY; ANDREW WAS A TRUSTEE AT THE TREADWELL METHODIST CHURCH AND HE AND HIS WIFE LED FAMILY BIBLE READINGS EVERY DAY. EDNA'S GRANDPARENTS, TOO, WERE VERY RELIGIOUS, AND HELEN PRIME RECALLS THAT AS A CHILD, HER FAVORITE BIBLE CLASS LEADER WAS DAVID GEORGIA.

"A KINDLY MAN, AND A SINCERE CHRISTIAN, HE DID NOT PRAY AS LONG AS WILLIAM FISHER, NOR AS LOUD AS HARTSON WHEAT, BUT HIS PRAYERS MADE ME WISH TO LIVE NEARER GOD," SHE SAID. "HE WAS HUMBLE BEFORE HIS MAKER, AND I HAD FAITH IN HIM."

DAVID'S AND LOVINA'S GRANDCHILDREN FOLLOWED IN DAVID'S FOOTSTEPS: WENDELL AS SUNDAY SCHOOL SUPERINTENDENT AND PRESIDENT OF THE CHURCH-AFFILIATED EPWORTH LEAGUE; EDNA AS A SUNDAY SCHOOL TEACHER, CHORISTER AND MEMBER OF THE SPRING LAKE MISSIONARY SOCIETY.

As a teenager, Edna attended Delaware Literary Institute nine miles away with Ethel Wheat of Treadwell, a friend from church. In February of 1907, Benedict was reported as having passed Regents examinations in arithmetic, U.S. history, physiology and drawing. Like her cousin, Grace Georgia, who taught at West Delhi, she became a teacher at L. B. Strong's District in 1911, and then at the Camp District, the Russell District and the Pines schools. She was hired for the latter position by her future father-in-law, school trustee Amzi Jonathan Benedict, who with his second wife, Sara Ackerley Benedict of Arena, had moved his family of three boys—Howard, Harry and Homer—from Meridale to Warner Hill Road in West Meredith in 1905.

Harry Benedict says it was probably at a Treadwell Methodist Church function that his brother, Howard Wesley Benedict, met neighbor Edna Georgia. Harry and Homer, nine and ten years younger than Howard, respectively, were students at the Pines School, District # 7, when Benedict taught there.

"There was a bar-way [a fence gate] in front of the school," recalls Harry. "I was 14 or 15 and I well remember the time she had ten or 12 of us kids get on our knees and put our heads through this bar-way and she took a picture of us. She also took one of us standing in front of the school. She would set the camera up on the tripod, and then put this dark cloth over her head to focus—she would do that several times, moving the camera around just so—and then the glass plates would be slid in the side of the camera. She would go under the cloth again and push the shutter release to take the picture."

After an engagement of about a year, Edna and Howard were married February 6, 1913 when he was 23 and she was 24, cutting short

HER TEACHING CAREER, AS MARRIED WOMEN WERE NOT ALLOWED TO TEACH SCHOOL. THEY RETAINED AN INTEREST IN AREA SCHOOLS, AND THE SCHOOLHOUSE ACROSS THE ROAD FROM THEIR FARM, ONCE CALLED THE LOU STRONG SCHOOL, WAS RE-NAMED THE HOWARD BENEDICT SCHOOL WHEN MR. BENEDICT WAS TRUSTEE.

HOWARD AND EDNA BOUGHT THE LOU STRONG FARM, KNOWN AS MAPLE ROW FARM, AT THE JUNCTION OF THE DELHI AND SUTHERLAND ROADS. THERE THEY RAISED JERSEY CATTLE AND LED AN ACTIVE, THOUGH CHILDLESS, LIFE. EDNA ENJOYED BAKING, PRESERVING FOODS AND DOING HANDICRAFTS, SUCH AS EMBROIDERY, SEWING AND TATTING. SHE SOMETIMES HELPED HOWARD ON THE FARM.

"HOT SUMMER DAYS WERE BUSY WITH HAYING AND THEN MILKING THE COWS," RECALLED NIECE CHRISTINA JONES. "TO SAVE TIME, AUNT EDNA WOULD SOMETIMES PACK A PICNIC SUPPER, COMPLETE WITH LEMONADE FROM FRESHLY SQUEEZED LEMONS. SHE WOULD MEET HOWARD IN THE HAY FIELD. SUPPER WOULD BE EATEN ON THE HAY SCATTERED OVER THE FLOOR OF THE HAYWAGON."

BENEDICT HAD MANY HOBBIES—SHE COLLECTED ANTIQUES AND HAVILAND CHINA, ENJOYED BICYCLING AND ICE SKATING, LOVED GROWING FLOWERS AND BIRD WATCHING. SHE OCCASIONALLY PHOTOGRAPHED THE WINGED VISITORS COAXED ONTO HOWARD'S FINGERS BY A COMBINATION OF HOME-MADE BIRD FEEDERS AND HER HUSBAND'S MIMICKING WHISTLES.

BENEDICT WAS ALSO AN AVID BASEBALL FAN. "SHE LISTENED BY RADIO TO THE WORLD SERIES EACH FALL," SAID CHRISTINA JONES. "SHE KEPT A TALLY OF RBIS, INNINGS AND SCORES. I WAS INVITED TO LISTEN AND KEEP SCORE FOR SEVERAL YEARS. I WOULD TAKE THE SCHOOLBUS TO AUNT EDNA'S AND FIND HER SEATED BY THE RADIO WITH A SCORECARD ALL PREPARED AHEAD OF TIME."

BENEDICT WAS ALSO A MEMBER OF THE WILLING WORKERS OF WEST MEREDITH, WHICH MET MONTHLY AS A SOCIAL AND PUBLIC SERVICE GROUP. THEY TIED OFF QUILTS, AND, DURING WORLD WAR II, MADE SHORT-FINGERED GUNNER'S MITTS FOR SERVICEMEN. EACH YEAR, AFTER THE FIRST CUTTING OF HAY, THE MEN, WOMEN AND CHILDREN OF THE GROUP WOULD GATHER AT THE CEMETERY JUST DOWN THE ROAD FROM THE GEORGIA HOMESTEAD, TRIM THE GRASS AND BRUSH AND THEN ENJOY A POTLUCK DINNER PUT TOGETHER BY THE WOMEN. THE WILLING WORKERS' MEETINGS AND ACTIVITIES WERE OFTEN THE SUBJECT OF EDNA BENEDICT'S PHOTOGRAPHS.

INDEED, BENEDICT'S LENS FOCUSED PREDOMINANTLY ON HER NEIGHBORS AND RELATIVES. HARRY BENEDICT REMEMBERS BEING PHOTOGRAPHED AS A TEENAGER WITH A YOUNG SPOTTED AYRSHIRE HE HAD RAISED FROM A CALF. "SHE GAVE ME THE PICTURE PRINTED ON A POSTCARD. I THOUGHT IT WAS A BIG DEAL," HE REMEMBERS.

ON ANOTHER OCCASION, EDNA PHOTOGRAPHED THE THREE BENEDICT BROTHERS, HOWARD, HARRY AND HOMER, ON THEIR FAMILY'S FARM. "WE DRESSED UP, WITH TIES AND SO ON, FOR THE PICTURE," WHICH WAS TAKEN INDOORS IN FRONT OF A PLAIN BACKGROUND, HARRY RECALLED.

HARRY, HIS WIFE VERNA MORRISON BENEDICT AND THEIR CHILDREN, ALTON, ELEANOR, DOROTHY, RALPH AND LYNN, LIVED ON A JERSEY FARM JUST DOWN WARNER HILL ROAD FROM EDNA AND HOWARD. HOMER, WHO WAS A TRAVELLING FARRIER AND ALSO DROVE A MILK TRUCK AND A SCHOOL BUS, LIVED IN SOUTH KORTRIGHT WITH WIFE ALICE JOHNSON BENEDICT AND THEIR CHILDREN CLAYTON AND EDWIN.

THOUGH THEY HAD NONE OF THEIR OWN, EDNA AND HOWARD LOVED CHILDREN AND WELCOMED THEM INTO THEIR HOME. "AS CHILDREN, MY SISTER AND I WERE OFTEN INVITED TO COME FOR A NIGHT," RELATED STEWART GEORGIA.

"Times of playing 'Touring,' 'Flinch,' and 'Chinese Checkers' are well remembered. For breakfast, we would generally have an egg poached in milk on toast." After breakfast, he says, there was usually a time for hymn-singing at the piano, and a Bible reading. During fishing season, Uncle Howard would bring the nieces and nephews along for a day of angling.

Picnics were another simple form of entertainment. "One I remember was near Delaware Academy, Delhi on an abandoned roadbed," says Christina Jones. "A fire was built and hotdogs roasted. The camera was tucked in with the food and a thick plaid wool blanket to sit on."

The Benedicts also enjoyed travelling further afield. They had grown up in an age when horse power was the four-legged kind. Indeed, the sight of a "horseless carriage" was considered news in 1907, when the *Delaware Dairyman* reported in its May 17 issue that "a large automobile passed through here last Sunday, just as people were coming to church."

Cars gradually replaced the horse as the principal means of transportation, however. Inspired by images of distant places they saw in the pages of *National Geographic*, and touched by a mutual case of wanderlust, Edna and Howard used their car to visit not only historic sites and places of interest in Delaware, Otsego and Greene Counties, but to see relatives in New Jersey, view the 1939 World's Fair in New York City, and, in 1940, to embark on a cross-country adventure.

"They were pioneer campers," says Christina Jones of the Benedicts' foray to California. They converted their car, a two-door sedan, into an early recreational vehicle. Edna, noted for her common sense and innovative approach to problems, "sewed cloth pockets with

ELASTIC TOPS TO THE SIDE OF THE CAR BY THE FRONT DOOR. THESE WERE HANDY PLACES FOR MAPS. THE BACK SEAT WAS REMOVED AND A MATTRESS FITTED FROM THE BACK OF THE FRONT SEAT INTO THE TRUNK. STORAGE AREAS WERE BUILT UNDER THE MATTRESS FOR FOOD AND CLOTHING. CAREFUL, COMPLETE RECORDS WERE KEPT OF GAS CONSUMPTION, OIL CHANGES AND EXPENSES." AND BENEDICT, OF COURSE, TOOK MANY PHOTOS OF THE WONDERS ALONG THE ROAD.

THE BENEDICTS' HEARTS REMAINED AT HOME, HOWEVER, WHERE THEY WERE ACTIVE IN THE AFFAIRS OF THE CHURCH, HOSTING SOCIALS AND PARTIES FOR THE EPWORTH LEAGUE AND OTHER GROUPS, AND TEACHING SUNDAY SCHOOL. THE TREADWELL METHODIST CHURCH HISTORY NOTES THAT HOWARD EVEN ORGANIZED A CHURCH SCHOOL CLASS FOR ADULTS AGED 18 TO 35. THE CLASS WAS DESCRIBED AS "ALERT AND QUESTIONING, FOR NOTHING IS ACCEPTED AS DOGMA."

THE BENEDICTS ARE REMEMBERED AS STRICT BUT FUN-LOVING. HOWARD HAD A QUICK WIT, AND HIS WIFE WAS OFTEN THE WILLING SUBJECT OF GOOD-NATURED TEASING. NONETHELESS, EDNA'S PHOTO SESSIONS WERE RECALLED BY STEWART GEORGIA AS "SOLEMN TIMES, AND SMILES WERE NOT OFTEN ENCOURAGED." DARKROOMS IN THE BASEMENT OF HER PARENTS' HOME, AND LATER IN THE FARMHOUSE SHE SHARED WITH HUSBAND HOWARD, WERE USED TO DEVELOP AND PRINT HER PHOTOS OF FRIENDS AND NEIGHBORS IN THE WEST MEREDITH-TREADWELL AREAS. HERS WAS NOT A COMMERCIAL ENTERPRISE, BUT SHE WAS INDEED SERIOUS ABOUT HER HOBBY, GIVEN THE MANY STEPS AND THE CHEMISTRY INVOLVED IN EXPOSING, DEVELOPING AND PRINTING GLASS PLATE NEGATIVES.

BENEDICT PURCHASED GLASS PLATES FROM STANLEY DRY PLATES OF NEWTON, MASSACHUSETTS, FROM THE SEARS-ROEBUCK CATALOGUE AND FROM THE DEFENDER PHOTO SUPPLY COMPANY IN ROCHESTER, NEW YORK, DEPENDING ON PRICES AND AVAILABILITY. IN A REFLECTION OF HER FRUGAL NATURE, SHE GAVE

REJECTED PHOTOGRAPHS, WHICH HAD BEEN PRINTED ON POSTCARD DEVELOPING PAPER, TO FAMILY MEMBERS FOR USE AS NOTECARDS.

EDNA BENEDICT ULTIMATELY EXCHANGED THE LABOR-INTENSIVE PRACTICE OF GLASS PLATE PHOTOGRAPHY FOR THE SIMPLICITY OF A KODAK BROWNIE BOX CAMERA AND OUTSIDE PROCESSING. SHE GRADUALLY STOPPED TAKING PHOTOGRAPHS ALTOGETHER.

ON APRIL 2, 1963, TWO MONTHS AFTER SHE AND HOWARD CELEBRATED THEIR GOLDEN WEDDING ANNIVERSARY, EDNA BENEDICT DIED OF A STROKE. SHE WAS 75 YEARS OLD. HOWARD PASSED AWAY IN 1983.

CHAPTER 6

THEIR LIVES REMEMBERED:

ANNA CARROLL

THE EMOTION IN THIS PHOTOGRAPH OF MOTHER AND BABY, TAKEN IN A HAMMOCK

ON THE FRONT LAWN, MAKES IT ESPECIALLY APPEALING.

IN THE ONLY KNOWN PHOTO CARROLL TOOK OF FARM LIFE, ETHEL AND GRACE KENNEY ARE SHOWN FEEDING THE CHICKENS.

THE SMALL WHITE FIGURE IS ENGULFED BY THE BRIDGE IN THIS PHOTO OF A

WOMAN ON A FOOTBRIDGE IN PRATTSVILLE, GREENE COUNTY.

CARROLL PHOTOGRAPHED HER BROTHER ADELBERT IN THE HAMMOCK ON THE
PORCH, WHICH SERVED AS AN INFORMAL STUDIO.

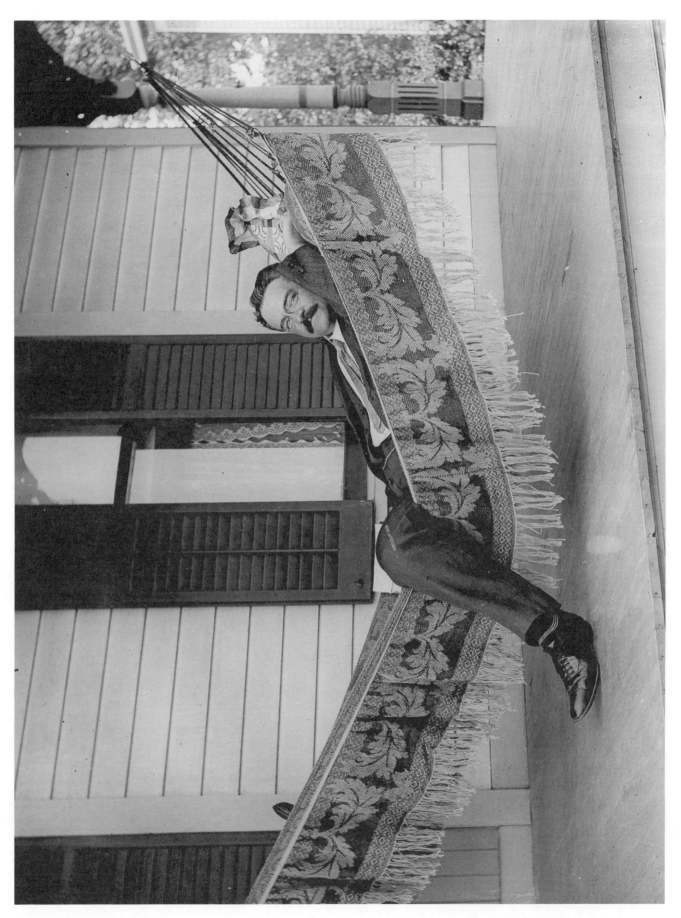

JESSIE CARROLL, SHOWN AT HER DESK IN HOBART, POSED WITH HER BACK TO THE

CAMERA IN THIS UNUSUAL PHOTOGRAPH.

IN THIS UNUSUAL INTERIOR SHOT OF A BEDROOM (SHADES DRAWN TO PREVENT
GLARE), ALL THE RUFFLES AND FLOURISHES OF A TYPICAL VICTORIAN HOME ARE
PRESENT.

THIS MAY BE A BRIDAL SHOWER OR A CHURCH BAZAAR. THERE ARE NO MEN

PRESENT. THIS INDOOR PHOTO GAVE CARROLL TROUBLE, AS LIGHT FROM THE

WINDOW OPPOSITE THE CAMERA CREATED A GLARE IN THE CENTER OF THE PICTURE.

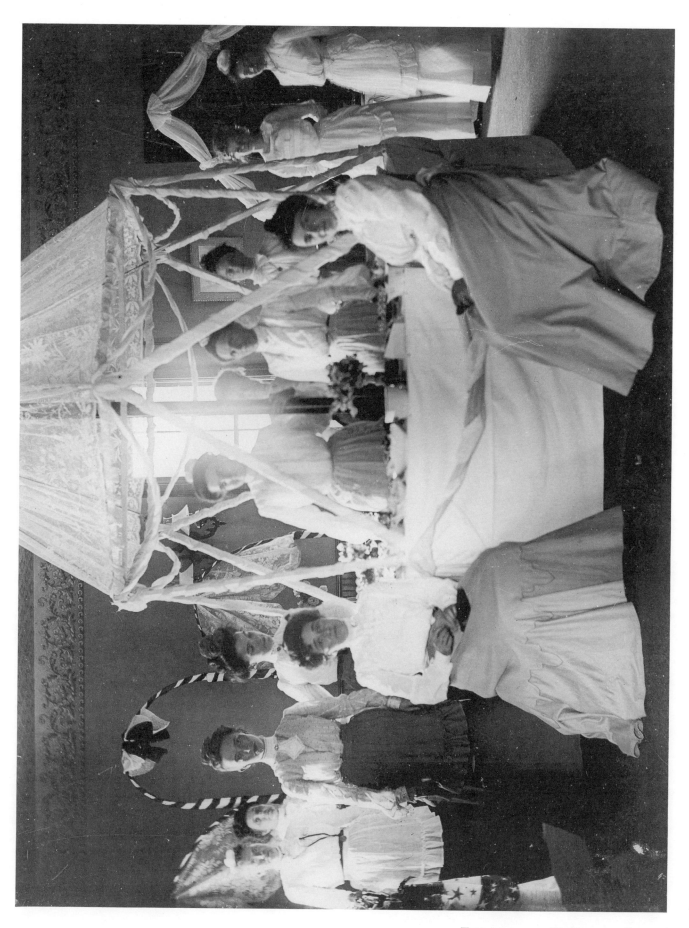

Avery "Doc" Hanford's croquet court was a popular place in Hobart.

Here, women in the community, including Mrs. Hanford, enjoy a game on

the Maple Street court.

COOKIES AND PUNCH WERE ENJOYED BY THIS HAPPY GROUP OF UNIDENTIFIED PICNICKERS, POSSIBLY A SUNDAY SCHOOL GROUP.

THIS GROUP OF CHILDREN, EITHER A CLASS FROM THE SCHOOL ACROSS THE STREET OR A SUNDAY SCHOOL CLASS, GATHERED ON A SLOPE AT ST. PETER'S EPISCOPAL CHURCH IN HOBART. JUDGING FROM THEIR SERIOUS EXPRESSIONS, THEY MUST HAVE BEEN TOLD NOT TO SMILE.

Several generations of women posed for this photo on the porch of a house on Maple Street, Hobart.

The separate spheres of men and women are subtly acknowledged in this beautifully balanced family photograph taken on a Hobart porch. The women are situated above the men and nearest the doorway, with the two young girls in the middle, one holding the family dog.

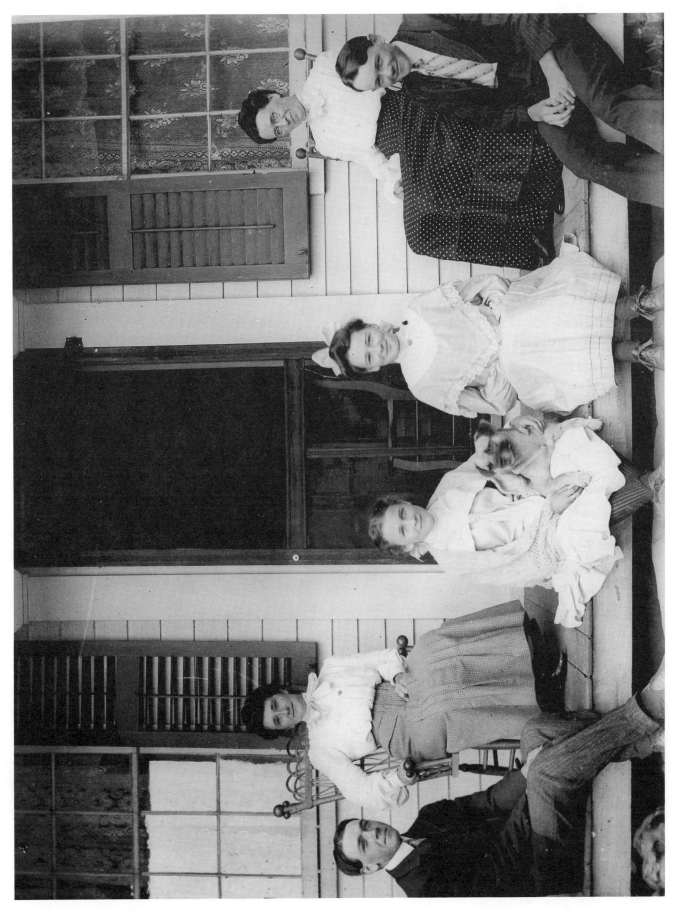

THE PORCH WAS A FAVORITE SETTING OF CARROLL'S. IT BRIDGED THE PRIVATE

REALM OF THE HOME WITH THE PUBLIC SPACE BEYOND. THE ELDERLY WOMAN

SEATED HERE WAS EVIDENTLY MISTRESS OF THIS STATELY HOME.

CARROLL AND A FRIEND IN HAMMOCK.

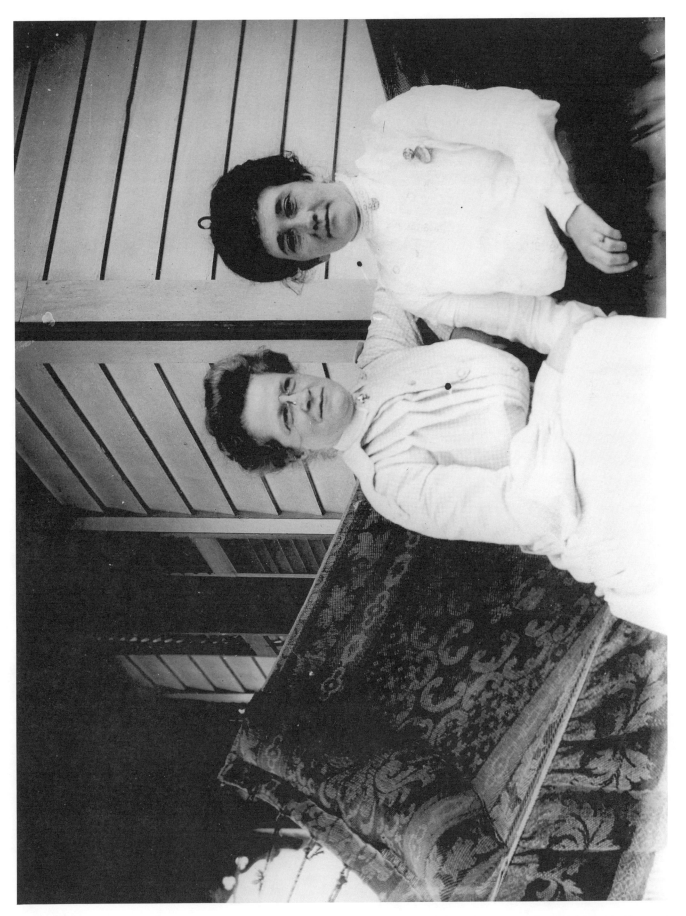

THIS PORTRAIT OF ETHEL IVES CANFIELD SHOWS CARROLL'S EYE FOR LINE AND CONTRAST AS SHE PLACED HER SUBJECT NEAR THE ANGLED TREE TO PROVIDE AN UNUSUAL BALANCE IN LIGHT AND DARK CONTRAST.

A TODDLER SNIFFING A DAHLIA REFLECTS THE INNOCENCE OF CHILDHOOD.

PROUD GRAND-DAD AND CURLY-HEADED INFANT ARE THE SUBJECTS IN THIS KEEPSAKE PORTRAIT.

JESSIE CARROLL AND SON CHARLES, PHOTOGRAPHED IN 1908, ARE THE PERFECT PICTURE OF MOTHER AND CHILD IN A TYPICAL VICTORIAN SETTING.

A WOMAN POSED SOLEMNLY WITH HER CATS IN A TYPICAL CENTERED, STRAIGHT-ON

PORTRAIT.

CARROLL USED PROPS—BABY SHOES, FLOWERS, A CHAIR—TO ENHANCE THIS

PHOTO OF MOTHER AND CHILD ON THE PORCH. A SCREEN WAS APPARENTLY PLACED

TO HIDE THE WINDOW IN THE BACKGROUND.

This young girl with her hoop may be dressed for a theatrical or athletic performance.

Anna Carroll

THE YEAR ANNA CARROLL WAS BORN—1868—WAS A CONVULSIVE ONE IN THE UNITED STATES. ANDREW JOHNSON BECAME THE FIRST PRESIDENT TO HAVE ARTICLES OF IMPEACHMENT BROUGHT AGAINST HIM AND ULYSSES S. GRANT WAS ELECTED HIS SUCCESSOR. THE 14TH AMENDMENT, GRANTING CITIZENSHIP TO FORMER SLAVES WAS ADOPTED, WHILE THE KU KLUX KLAN INVIGORATED ITS EFFORTS TO REGAIN WHITE SUPREMACY IN THE SOUTH. SUSAN B. ANTHONY FORMED THE SUFFRAGETTE NEWSPAPER, *THE REVOLUTION*, WHOSE MOTTO WAS "THE TRUE REPUBLIC-MEN, THEIR RIGHTS AND NOTHING MORE; WOMEN, THEIR RIGHTS AND NOTHING LESS."

THE SPORT OF VELOCIPEDING (CYCLING), IMPORTED FROM FRANCE, WAS IN VOGUE, AND LOUISA MAY ALCOTT PUBLISHED *LITTLE WOMEN*, WHICH WAS TO BECOME THE MOST POPULAR GIRL'S STORY IN AMERICAN LITERATURE, SELLING MORE THAN 2,000,000 COPIES.

IN ROCHESTER, NEW YORK, 50,000 VISITORS ATTENDED THE ANNUAL AGRICULTURAL FAIR, WHERE THEY NO DOUBT LEARNED ABOUT A NEW ORGANIZATION OF AMERICAN FARMERS—THE NATIONAL GRANGE OF THE PATRONS OF HUSBANDRY (OR, SIMPLY, THE GRANGE). ESTABLISHED A YEAR EARLIER AS AN EDUCATIONAL AND SOCIAL GROUP, THE GRANGE SOON BECAME POLITICALLY ACTIVE, AND BY 1875, HAD 858,000 MEMBERS NATIONWIDE.

THIS WAS THE WORLD INTO WHICH ANNA CARROLL WAS BORN SEPTEMBER 25, 1868 IN THE TOWN OF ROXBURY. ANNA WAS ONE OF FIVE CHILDREN OF SAMUEL B. AND ELSIE TRAVIS CARROLL, WHO LIVED ON A FARM ON NEW KINGSTON ROAD OFF MEEKER HOLLOW.

BOTH OF CARROLL'S PARENTS WERE BORN OF MEEKER HOLLOW PIONEERS: ELSIE (OR ELSA) WAS ONE OF 11 CHILDREN OF ETHIEL AND SALACHA TRAVIS, AND SAMUEL WAS ONE OF FIVE OFFSPRING OF ENOS AND ANNA STRATTON CARROLL. NEIGHBORS ELSA AND SAMUEL WERE MARRIED IN 1853 AND BEGAN A FAMILY THAT INCLUDED FOUR CHILDREN: ARNOLD S., ADELBERT E., ANNA S., NAMED FOR HER GRANDMOTHER, AND ABBIE.

LITTLE IS KNOWN OF CARROLL'S EARLY LIFE ON THE FARM. HER FATHER DIED WHEN SHE WAS JUST 16, AND FOUR YEARS LATER, IN 1888, HER MOTHER WAS MARRIED AGAIN, TO EDWARD FAULKNER OF ROXBURY, WHO DIED IN 1893. (IN 1901, THE CARROLL FAMILY SOLD THEIR ROXBURY FARM TO ALBERT KOUTZ, A GERMAN IMMIGRANT, AND IT LATER BECAME PART OF WHAT IS NOW THE MANHATTAN COUNTRY SCHOOL FARM.)

IN ABOUT 1895 CARROLL, WHOSE SIBLINGS HAD MARRIED OR LEFT HOME, MOVED WITH HER MOTHER TO HOBART, WHERE HER BROTHER ARNOLD HAD A HARDWARE AND CUTLERY STORE. THERE THE TWO WOMEN SET UP HOUSEKEEPING AT MAPLE PARK, AND BECAME PART OF A THRIVING COMMUNITY KNOWN FOR ITS BUSTLING INDUSTRIES, ITS RAIL-FED TOURIST TRADE AND ITS "REFINED"—AND ALCOHOL-FREE—ATMOSPHERE.

ORIGINALLY KNOWN AS WATERTOWN BECAUSE THE WEST BRANCH OF THE DELAWARE RIVER FLOWED DIRECTLY THROUGH TOWN, HOBART WAS ALSO CALLED TINKERTOWN IN ITS EARLY DAYS, BECAUSE OF THE MANY WATER-POWERED ENTERPRISES THAT SPRANG UP ALONG THE RIVER AND ITS TRIBUTARIES. LATER NAMED FOR ROBERT SMITH HOBART, BISHOP OF THE EPISCOPAL CHURCH, THE HAMLET GREW TO MORE THAN 600 PEOPLE. IN 1896, MANY OF THEM FOUND WORK AT JOHN ROBINSON'S FOUNDRY AND MACHINE SHOP, OR GEORGE YOUNG'S HOBART MILLS, DEALERS IN FLOUR, FEED, LUMBER, COAL AND CEMENT, OR WITH THE ULSTER & DELAWARE RAILROAD OR THE HOTELS CATERING TO ITS TRAVELERS.

Farms surrounding the hamlet did much of their business in Hobart—they brought their milk to the Halsey-Sheffield Farm Creamery, got cider barrels made at John Bush's cooper shop, had their horses shod at Barlow & Butler blacksmiths, and got their wagons repaired at VanDusen & Hoyt.

There were four dressmakers, two milliners and as many shoemakers, two jewelry stores, a couple of drug stores and various dry-goods establishments. Arnold Carroll even had competition for his hardware store from F. G. Silliman. But there were apparently no commercial photographers in Hobart in 1896 when Anna Carroll stepped in to fill the void, becoming Hobart's unofficial community chronicler.

"She took pictures of her friends and relatives," recounted great-niece Eleanor Carroll Dye. "Her photography almost became more than a hobby. She was so good at it, it became a regular part of her life."

With her red-orange hair and her ever-present camera and tripod, Anna Carroll became a familiar sight on the streets of Hobart, where she photographed lawn parties and school students, shops and scenic views. This was an era when "Roman knife-throwing" might be the feature at a community entertainment, when organ grinders showed up on the street and when candy pulls and garden parties were common.

Carroll was there to record matches on the croquet court of Avery "Doc" Hanford, who opened the court to the public—men, women and children, too. She was on hand for functions at the Methodist Church of which she was a very active member. Perhaps she was present with camera in hand when the Ladies Social Circle of the Methodist Church gave a turkey supper in November of 1900, raising $80.50, and

WHEN BROTHER ARNOLD'S WIFE ELEANOR KALTENBACH CARROLL HOSTED A SOCIAL FOR THE LADIES MISSIONARY SOCIETY IN MARCH OF 1901.

ALTHOUGH SHE IS REMEMBERED AS BEING VERY ATTRACTIVE AND ENERGETIC, SHE APPARENTLY DID NOT HAVE MANY SUITORS, AND SO DEVOTED HERSELF TO CARING FOR HER AGED MOTHER, TENDING TO THEIR HOME, AND ENGAGING IN CREATIVE HOBBIES. "SHE WAS VERY ARTISTIC. SHE PAINTED WITH OILS AND WATER-COLORS, MADE BASKETS, PAINTED CHINA, PLAYED PIANO, ALL THE THINGS THAT WERE EXPECTED OF A LEISURED, TALENTED WOMAN," SAYS GREAT-NIECE ELEANOR CARROLL DYE. SHE HAD TIME TO PURSUE PHOTOGRAPHY, WHICH MRS. DYE CALLED "A NATURAL EXTENSION OF HER TALENTS. SHE HAD A SENSE OF COMPOSITION."

SHE ALSO HAD A SENSE OF HUMOR, ACCORDING TO JOHN JACKSON OF JEFFERSON, NEW YORK WHO ACQUIRED NEARLY 500 OF ANNA CARROLL'S GLASS PLATE NEGATIVES AFTER THEY WERE FOUND IN THE ATTIC OF HER FORMER HOME SEVERAL YEARS AGO. "WHEN I HELD SOME OF THE NEGATIVES UP TO THE LIGHT, ONE OF THE FIRST I SAW WAS A LADY WITH AN ALLIGATOR, AND I THOUGHT, 'THIS LOOKS LIKE FUN!'," MR. JACKSON SAID. ANOTHER PLATE SHOWED A GROUP OF 12 TO 15 PEOPLE POSING ON THE LAWN. A GENTLEMAN IN THE FRONT ROW WAS WEARING A HAT WITH AN APPLE ON IT. "I DON'T THINK HE PUT IT THERE, BECAUSE THERE'S A TEENAGER BEHIND HIM OBVIOUSLY TRYING TO KEEP A STRAIGHT FACE, AND THE WOMEN MUST HAVE BEEN GIGGLING, BECAUSE THEY HAD MOVED, CREATING A BLUR." ANNA MUST HAVE SEEN THE PRANK AS SHE FOCUSED AND THEN TOOK THE PICTURE, BUT SHE TOOK IT ANYWAY.

CARROLL LOVED CHILDREN, AND WITH NONE OF HER OWN, DOTED ON HER CHARGES AT SUNDAY SCHOOL, AND ON HER NIECES AND NEPHEWS. SISTER ABBIE AND HUSBAND HENRY COWAN HAD FIVE CHILDREN AND LIVED NEARBY. ARNOLD AND ELEANOR CARROLL HAD ONE SON ISAAC. THEY WERE FREQUENT VISITORS AT

THE HOME OF ANNA AND HER MOTHER. ADELBERT CARROLL, WHO LIVED IN SARATOGA, ALSO VISITED DURING THE SUMMER AND ON SPECIAL OCCASIONS.

So, EVEN AFTER HER MOTHER ELSIE CARROLL FAULKNER DIED ON JUNE 2, 1909, CARROLL WAS NEVER FAR FROM COMPANY. SHE WAS VERY ACTIVE WITH THE HOBART CIVIC CLUB, ESTABLISHED IN 1908 AS THE FEMALE COUNTERPART TO THE ALL-MALE CITIZEN'S ASSOCIATION, WHICH HAD ABOUT 70 MEMBERS. THE *STAMFORD MIRROR-RECORDER* OF MARCH 18 THAT YEAR REPORTED THAT THE CIVIC CLUB "HELD ANOTHER MEETING TUESDAY EVENING. THE LADIES ARE TAKING HOLD OF THIS WORK IN EARNEST AND IT ALREADY BIDS FAIR TO RIVAL THE MEN'S BUSINESS ASSOCIATION."

IT'S NOT CLEAR WHAT THE CIVIC CLUB DID WITH THE MONEY IT RAISED THROUGH DINNERS, WHITE SALES AND THE LIKE. BUT IT ALSO CONDUCTED COMMUNITY SINGS AND OTHER EVENTS, INCLUDING, IN 1915, PERFORMANCES BY THE CHICAGO MUSICAL CLUB, THE ROYAL MALE QUARTET AND THE MASON JUBILEE SINGERS. LECTURER ROBERT MILES ALSO GAVE A PUBLIC TALK UNDER THE CLUB'S AUSPICES.

THE MEN'S GROUP, TOO, BROUGHT IN ENTERTAINERS, AND WORKED TO PROMOTE THE TOWN. IN A 1913 BROCHURE, THE ASSOCIATION POINTED OUT THAT "NO INTOXICANTS ARE SOLD HERE, AND GREAT CARE IS TAKEN TO MAKE THE PLACE ATTRACTIVE TO A REFINED AND CULTIVATED CLASS OF PEOPLE."

THE EFFORT TO KEEP HOBART DRY HAD BEEN GOING ON FOR SOME TIME. IT'S NOT KNOWN HOW ANNA FELT ABOUT IT, BUT HER SISTER-IN-LAW, ELEANOR CARROLL, WAS SECRETARY OF THE HOBART CHAPTER OF THE WOMEN'S CHRISTIAN TEMPERANCE UNION. THE WCTU INVITED A PROFESSOR HOPKINS TO LECTURE ON THE EVILS OF DRINK IN FEBRUARY OF 1901, WHEN THE COMMUNITY WAS DEBATING WHETHER TO LICENSE ESTABLISHMENTS FOR THE SALE OF ALCOHOL.

In the February 16, 1901 issue of the *Mirror-Recorder*, the writer of an article on a fire at St. Peter's Episcopal Church in Hobart used the occasion to state his or her opinion on the licensing issue. The landmark church, the article said, "would seem to hide herself in ashes before witnessing the crowning of the century with the free sale of rum in town."

But the town remained dry, its inhabitants preferring to take their fun (in public, anyway) without alcohol. On November 4, 1908, "the young people of the high school gave a husking bee at the Civic Club rooms that furnished a good time to all." There were "moving pictures" at Grant's Opera House, and private parties hosted by local residents, including Carroll.

In July of 1915, for example, Carroll and her niece, Isaac's wife Jessie, "entertained a number of ladies informally." Jessie was spending the summer with her aunt while Isaac, school superintendent at Oswego, New York, was taking graduate courses at Columbia University in New York City. Isaac and Jessie's three children, Charles, Frederick and Eleanor, would, in their turn, become the subject of some of Carroll's photographs. Eleanor would always remember her great-aunt's mysterious disappearances beneath the black focusing cloth of the camera attached to its tripod.

Whether posed on a grassy hill at school, or on a hay wagon, or sniffing flowers in their own backyards, children were a favorite subject of Anna Carroll's. Her keepsake photo of a child at his first birthday party, angelic against the pure white of the tablecloth and the

DARK TREES BEHIND, IS AN OUTSTANDING EXAMPLE OF HER SENSITIVE APPROACH TO PHOTOGRAPHING CHILDREN.

AS HAS BEEN SAID, ANNA DID NOT ATTEMPT TO USE HER CRAFT TO SHAKE UP THE SOCIETY IN WHICH SHE LIVED, BUT CHOSE RATHER TO UPHOLD THE VICTORIAN VALUES WITH WHICH SHE WAS RAISED. ONE EXAMPLE IS A PHOTOGRAPH SHE TOOK OF JESSIE CARROLL WRITING AT HER DESK. THE PHOTO, WHICH WAS IN ALL LIKELIHOOD STAGED, IDEALIZES THE LEISURED WOMAN, PENNING A MISSIVE TO A FRIEND OR RELATIVE WITH TEAPOT CLOSE AT HAND, PHOTOGRAPHS AND OTHER MEMENTOS ON THE WALL NEARBY.

AT THE TURN OF THE CENTURY, MUCH SOCIALIZING OCCURRED ON THE FRONT PORCH, A PLACE TO SEE AND BE SEEN, A PHYSICAL AND EMOTIONAL EXTENSION OF A WOMAN'S DOMESTIC SPHERE. ANNA OFTEN USED HER FRONT PORCH AND THOSE OF HER NEIGHBORS AS A PHOTOGRAPHIC STUDIO. SHE COULD USE NATURAL LIGHT, AND HER SUBJECTS FELT AND LOOKED MORE COMFORTABLE IN THIS RELAXED SETTING. THE PHOTO OF HER BROTHER ADELBERT STRETCHED OUT ON THE PORCH HAMMOCK AFTER THE LONG JOURNEY FROM SARATOGA IS ONE EXAMPLE OF THIS; A SHOT OF AN UNIDENTIFIED WOMAN WITH HER PET CATS ON THE PORCH STEPS IS ANOTHER.

CARROLL IS BELIEVED TO HAVE DONE HER OWN FILM DEVELOPING AND PRINT PROCESSING. BUT WE KNOW NOTHING OF HER DARKROOM AND LITTLE ABOUT THE EQUIPMENT AND MATERIAL SHE USED. THE ONLY DOCUMENT WHICH SPEAKS OF ANY OF HER PURCHASES OF PHOTOGRAPHIC SUPPLIES IS A LETTER SHE WROTE JANUARY 26, 1903 TO THE DEFENDER PHOTO SUPPLY COMPANY IN ROCHESTER, NEW YORK ASKING FOR PRODUCT DESCRIPTIONS AND PRICE LISTS.

THE MOST PRODUCTIVE TIME OF CARROLL'S LIFE, AS FAR AS HER PHOTOGRAPHY WAS CONCERNED, WERE THE YEARS BETWEEN 1904 AND 1910, THOUGH SHE CONTINUED TO TAKE PICTURES UNTIL THE EARLY 1920s. SHE DIED UNEXPECTEDLY AUGUST 2, 1925 OF PNEUMONIA FOLLOWING GALL BLADDER SURGERY. ANNA CARROLL WAS SO REVERED IN HER COMMUNITY THAT A STAINED GLASS WINDOW WAS INSTALLED IN HER MEMORY IN THE METHODIST CHURCH.

WE CANNOT TELL WHAT PROMPTED ANNA CARROLL TO DELVE INTO PHOTOGRAPHY, NOR HOW SHE LEARNED THE CRAFT. WE KNOW ONLY THE BAREST ESSENTIALS ABOUT HOW SHE TOOK HER PHOTOGRAPHS, AND NOT MUCH MORE ABOUT WHY. PERHAPS JOHN JACKSON'S SIMPLE THEORY IS BEST: "SHE DID IT BECAUSE SHE LOVED IT. AND I'M GLAD SHE HAD AN INTEREST IN PHOTOGRAPHY, BECAUSE SHE WAS ABLE TO CAPTURE, IN AN ARTFUL WAY, THE FLAVOR OF THAT TIME IN HISTORY."

CHAPTER 7

THEIR WORK CONSIDERED

 THEY WERE NOT THE ONLY WOMEN IN RURAL DELAWARE COUNTY TO TAKE UP PHOTOGRAPHY IN ITS EARLY DAYS, FOR IT WAS A HOBBY THAT APPEALED TO MILLIONS AND CROSSED LINES OF GENDER, OCCUPATION AND SOCIAL STATUS.

NOR WERE THEY IN THE SAME LEAGUE AS CONTEMPORARIES LEWIS HINE, ALFRED STEIGLITZ, JULIA MARGARET CAMERON OR GERTRUDE KASEBIER, WHOSE PHOTOGRAPHS HAVE BEEN WIDELY PUBLISHED AND EXAMINED AS FINE ART.

NEVERTHELESS, THE PHOTOGRAPHS OF ANNA CARROLL, EDNA BENEDICT AND LENA UNDERWOOD DESERVE OUR ATTENTION AND ADMIRATION FOR A NUMBER OF REASONS.

FIRST, THEY REPRESENT LARGE, SUBSTANTIALLY INTACT BODIES OF WORK WITH NAMES ATTACHED. THEY ARE NOT ANONYMOUS. WE KNOW WHO TOOK THESE PHOTOS, AND THEREFORE WE LEARN SOMETHING ABOUT THE PHOTOGRAPHERS AS WE STUDY THE IMAGES THEY LEFT US.

SECOND, MANY OF THESE PHOTOGRAPHS ARE DOCUMENTARY IN NATURE. CAPTURING A MOMENT IN HISTORY FOR POSTERITY IS ITSELF A SIGNIFICANT CONTRIBUTION. CARROLL'S PORTRAIT OF A YOUNG GIRL WITH A HOOP, FOR EXAMPLE, DEPICTS A LONG-LOST CHILDHOOD PAST-TIME. BENEDICT'S LANDSCAPE OF A HILLSIDE CLEARED TO ITS SUMMIT, CRISS-CROSSED WITH STONE WALLS, WILL

NEVER AGAIN LOOK THAT WAY, AS IT HAS SINCE BEEN RE-FORESTED. UNDERWOOD'S WINTERTIME VIEW OF MAIN STREET IN ROXBURY MAY HAVE BEEN INTENDED TO SHOW THE DEPTH OF NEW-FALLEN SNOW, BUT IS OF INTEREST TO US TODAY BECAUSE OF THE STRUCTURES AND BUSINESSES THAT NO LONGER EXIST.

BEYOND THIS, THE THREE COLLECTIONS ARE INTRIGUING FOR THEIR DISTINCTIVE APPROACHES.

ANNA CARROLL'S EYE WAS VERY MUCH A FEMININE ONE, FOCUSING PRIMARILY ON DOMESTIC LIFE, AND ALMOST EXCLUSIVELY ON OTHER WOMEN AND THEIR CHILDREN. USING ARTFUL COMBINATIONS OF LIGHT AND SETTING, HER PHOTOS OFTEN DEPICT AN IDEALIZED VERSION OF FAMILY LIFE.

EDNA BENEDICT'S WORK WAS RATHER LESS CONSIDERED, AND MORE SPONTANEOUS, OR AS SPONTANEOUS AS COULD BE MANAGED GIVEN THE CUMBERSOME NATURE OF THE PHOTOGRAPHIC PROCESS AT THE TIME. HER PICTURES ARE ALSO MORE COMMUNITY-ORIENTED, THEIR SUBJECTS MORE IMPORTANT TO HER THAN THE TECHNIQUE EMPLOYED TO PHOTOGRAPH THEM.

LENA UNDERWOOD, WORKING YEARS LATER THAN ANNA AND EDNA, TOOK ADVANTAGE OF ADVANCES IN FILM AND EQUIPMENT TO CONCENTRATE ON COMPOSITION AND THE ABILITY OF A PHOTO TO TELL A STORY. SHE ALSO WENT A STEP FURTHER, EMPLOYING AN EYE FOR COLOR IN THE HAND-PAINTING OF MANY OF HER BLACK AND WHITE PRINTS.

CARROLL, WHO WAS VERY AWARE OF HOW A SUBJECT'S SURROUNDINGS CREATED A MOOD, WORKED TO *MAKE* HER PHOTOGRAPHS, AS OPPOSED TO SIMPLY DOCUMENTING A SCENE. TAKE, FOR EXAMPLE, THE FAMILY PHOTOGRAPHED ON THEIR FRONT PORCH, WOMEN AT EACH SIDE OF THE DOOR, CHILDREN IN THE CENTER, MEN FRAMING THE GROUP. THIS ARRANGEMENT SPEAKS VOLUMES ABOUT THE ACCEPTED ROLES OF FAMILY MEMBERS AT THE TIME.

The more memorable of her photos were clearly not happenstance. In the portrait of a mother and child seated on a hammock, for instance, Anna kept background distractions to a minimum in this home setting, and perhaps went so far as to suggest her subjects' complementary white gowns. The mother was instructed to hold the infant close to her—an effort was made to create an image of inseparability, what women's historian Josephine Gear calls "baby worship and the adulation of the mother."

Perhaps because she was unmarried and had no children of her own, Anna Carroll seemed to take special pains with her photographs of infants and youngsters, creating intimate mementos for their families. A photograph of a toddler sniffing a dahlia from an immense bush offers an image of youthful innocence sampling the fruits of nature.

Her photos of adults, while occasionally whimsical, are more often elegant, almost contrived. A photograph of a woman in a beautiful white dress standing in the middle of a suspension footbridge juxtaposes human fragility with pastoral splendor. The viewer's eye flows from left to right, following the swooping lines of the bridge to the small figure at center.

Edna Benedict's work, by contrast, was less sophisticated. While Carroll's work reflected her personal vision of what life should be, Benedict photographed life as she saw it, although in a generally positive light. The sheer volume of photographs she produced is an indication of how important the act of documenting her community was to her. But in most of those photos, the people in them don't carry any more weight than the horses or the landscape or the buildings.

There are examples, however, of how she utilized the background

TO HELP TELL THE STORY. ONE SUCH PHOTO SHOWS A MAN PUTTING A LILAC IN A WOMAN'S HAIR. THE COUPLE STANDS BENEATH A TOWERING LILAC BUSH, SOMEWHAT DWARFED, BUT OBVIOUSLY ENJOYING THE MOMENT, AS WE DO VICARIOUSLY.

LESS TECHNICALLY ACCOMPLISHED THAN EITHER CARROLL OR UNDERWOOD, BENEDICT'S COLLECTION SHOWS MISTAKES IN JUDGEMENT AND PROCESSING, LIKE THE PHOTO OF A FAMILY GROUPED IN THE SHADE IN FRONT OF THEIR HOME. THEIR FACES ARE ALL BUT OBSCURED BY THE CONTRAST CREATED FROM A CIRCLE OF SUNLIGHT BETWEEN THEM AND THE CAMERA. THEN THERE ARE SUCCESSFUL USES OF SUCH CONTRAST, AS IN THE PHOTOGRAPH OF THE GIRLS, DRESSED IN WHITE FROM HEAD TO TOE, APPEARING ALMOST TRANSLUCENT AMIDST A BACKGROUND OF DARK FOLIAGE.

LENA UNDERWOOD, LIKE ANNA CARROLL, SHOWED A PROCLIVITY FOR PHOTOGRAPHING CHILDREN—HER OWN. MANY OF THOSE PHOTOS WERE CAREFULLY CRAFTED TO PRODUCE A DESIRED IMAGE OR EFFECT. BUT SOME, AS UNREHEARSED AS CHILDREN'S LIVES, ARE ALL THE MORE MEMORABLE FOR THEIR SPONTANEOUS NATURE. SPOTTING ONE OF HER SONS SLUMPED ASLEEP IN AN INFANT SWING HANGING FROM A PORCH CEILING, LENA CHOSE AN UNUSUAL PERSPECTIVE FOR A PHOTOGRAPH OF THIS SCENE, FAMILIAR TO MOST PARENTS—SHE EITHER LAID DOWN ON THE PORCH FLOOR OR PLACED THE CAMERA THERE TO RECORD THE VIEW LOOKING SLIGHTLY UPWARD AT THE CHILD.

ANOTHER UNEXPECTED PHOTOGRAPH SHOWS SON DAN HOISTING AN APPARENTLY UNCOMPLAINING CAT BY THE BELLY, AS TODDLERS ARE WONT TO DO. THE FACT THAT THE PHOTO IS SLIGHTLY OUT OF FOCUS DOES NOT REALLY DETRACT FROM ITS APPEAL. IN FACT, IT WAS EVIDENTLY ONE OF THE PHOTOGRAPHER'S FAVORITES, AS SHE CHOSE TO HAND-COLOR AN ENLARGED PRINT OF IT.

LENA UNDERWOOD OBVIOUSLY ENJOYED EXPERIMENTING WITH

COMPOSITION AND COLOR. ONE OF HER HAND-PAINTED PHOTOS SHOWS HER BOYS SLEDDING WITH THEIR BLACK AND WHITE DOG. SHE TOOK THE PHOTO FROM A DISTANCE, WITH BARE BRUSH IN THE FOREGROUND, A STARK TREE ON A HILLSIDE BEHIND, THE BOYS' HEADS AND FEET THE ONLY PARTS OF THEIR BODIES SHOWING ABOVE THE BANK OF SNOW AS THEY CAREENED DOWN A HILL ON THEIR BELLIES. THE FROLICKING DOG IS A BLUR OF MOTION.

IN A PHOTOGRAPH WHICH MIGHT HAVE SIMPLY RECORDED THE EXISTENCE OF A ROOT CELLAR IN A HILLSIDE BENEATH A SPREADING TREE, THE PRESENCE OF THE TOPS OF SEVERAL FLOWERS IN THE LOWER RIGHT CORNER—PAINTED IN SHADES OF BLUE, YELLOW AND PINK—ARE A WELCOME SURPRISE IN AN OTHERWISE ALL-GREEN SCENE.

WHATEVER THEIR INDIVIDUAL ACHIEVEMENTS, HOWEVER, THESE THREE WOMEN ALL SEEMED IMPLICITLY TO UNDERSTAND THE POWER OF PHOTOGRAPHY. THEY RECOGNIZED THAT MEMORIES—BOTH PERSONAL AND COMMUNAL—ARE DEFINED AND PRESERVED THROUGH PHOTOGRAPHS.

PRACTICING PHOTOGRAPHY YEARS BEFORE TECHNOLOGICAL ADVANCES AND POPULAR CUSTOM MADE THE MEDIUM AN ENDEMIC AND UNIVERSAL PART OF PRIVATE AND PUBLIC LIFE, CARROLL, BENEDICT AND UNDERWOOD UNCONSCIOUSLY, PERHAPS, EXPANDED THE ROLE OF THE CAMERA IN THEIR LIVES AND COMMUNITIES, EVEN AS THEY SIMULTANEOUSLY EXPANDED THEIR OWN ROLE AS WOMEN WITHIN THOSE COMMUNITIES.

THE PHOTOGRAPHS THEY LEFT BEHIND ARE A FASCINATING DOCUMENT OF THE VALUES AND ACTIVITIES OF THE PEOPLE THEY KNEW AND OF THEMSELVES. TO PARAPHRASE HISTORIAN ALAN TRACHTENBERG, THROUGH THEIR PHOTOGRAPHS— AND THE EYE OF EACH WOMAN BEHIND THE CAMERA—WE ARE ABLE TO MAKE THE RANDOM, FRAGMENTARY, AND ACCIDENTAL DETAILS OF THEIR EVERYDAY EXISTENCE MEANINGFUL.

BIBLIOGRAPHY

"A Souvenir of Old St. Peter's and of Hobart Village." Hobart, New York: Independent Press, 1905.

Arnheim, Rudolf. *Art and Visual Perception: A Psychology of the Creative Eye.* Berkeley: University of California Press, 1957.

Banta, Martha. *Imaging American Women.* New York: Columbia University Press, 1987.

Barnes, Catharine Weed. "Women as Photographers." *The Photographic Times and American Photographer* 17 (March 18, 1887): 275-278.

Barnes, Catharine Weed. "Photography from a Woman's Standpoint. " *Anthony's Photographic Bulletin* 21 (January 25, 1890): 39-42. In Peter Palmquist, ed. *Camera Fiends & Kodak Girls: 50 Selections by and About Women in Photography, 1840-1930.* New York: Midmarch Arts Press, 1989.

Biographical Review Publishing Company. *The Leading Citizens of Delaware County, New York.* Boston, 1895.

Braden, Donna R. *Leisure and Entertainment in America.* Dearborn, Michigan: Henry Ford Museum and and Greenfield Village, 1988.

Citizens' Association Hobart, New York, The. *Hobart-In-The-Catskills, New York.* 1913.

Coe, Brian and Paul Gates. *The Snapshot Photograph: The Rise of Popular Photography 1888-1939.* London: Ash & Grant, 1977.

Cook, Ina L. "The Camera and the Child." *Camera Club* (September 1913): 442. In Peter Palmquist, *Shadowcatchers: A Directory of Women in California Photography 1900-1920.* Arcata, California: 1990. 76-78.

Corwin, E.A. Mrs. "The Camera in the Home." *Camera Craft* (November 1910): 403-408. In Peter Palmquist, *Shadowcatchers: A Directory of Women in California Photography 1900-1920.* Arcata, California: 1990. 79-81.

Delaware County Historical Association. *Two Stones for Every Dirt: The Story of Delaware County, New York.* Fleischmanns, New York: Purple Mountain Press, Ltd., 1987.

De Vine, John F. *Three Centuries in Delaware County, New York.* New York: Swiss Alps of Delaware County, 1933.

Edgerton, Giles. [Mary Fanton Roberts]. "Photography as an Emotional Art: A study of the Work of Gertrude Kasebier." *The Craftsman.* (April 13, 1907): 80-93. Also in Peter Palmquist, ed. *Camera Fiends & Kodak Girls: 50 Selections by and About Women in Photography, 1840 - 1930.* New York: Midmarch Arts Press, 1989, 171-180.

Gear, Josephine. "The Baby's Picture: Woman as Image Maker in Small Town America." *Feminist Studies* (Summer 1987) 419-42.

Gilbert, George. *More Photographic Advertising From A-To-Z: From the Kodak to the Leica, Volume Two.* New York: Portertown Products, Inc., 1975.

Gover, Jane C. *The Positive Image: Women Photographers in Turn of the Century America.* Albany: State University of New York Press, 1988.

GREENOUGH, SARAH, JOEL SNYDER, DAVID TRAVIS, COLIN WESTERBECK. *ON THE ART OF FIXING A SHADOW.* NATIONAL GALLERY OF ART AND THE ART INSTITUTE OF CHICAGO, 1989.

GRIFFIN, IRMA MAE. *THE HISTORY OF THE TOWN OF ROXBURY.* REVISED EDITION, DELHI, NEW YORK: PRIVATELY PRINTED, 1975.

GUTMAN, JUDITH MARA. "FAMILY PHOTO INTERPRETATION." *KIN AND COMMUNITIES: FAMILIES IN AMERICA.* WASHINGTON, D.C.: SMITHSONIAN INSTITUTION PRESS, 1976.

HARRIS, BARBARA J. *BEYOND HER SPHERE: WOMEN AND THE PROFESSIONS IN AMERICAN HISTORY* WESTPORT, CONNECTICUT: GREENWOOD PRESS, 1978.

HILLEBRAND, PAMELA S. *TREASURES OF THE ONE ROOM SCHOOL.* DELAWARE COUNTY, NEW YORK: 1988.

HIRSCH, JULIA. *FAMILY PHOTOGRAPHS: CONTENT, MEANING AND EFFECT.* NEW YORK: OXFORD UNIVERSITY PRESS, 1981.

HISTORY OF DELAWARE COUNTY WITH ILLUSTRATIONS, BIOGRAPHICAL SKETCHES AND PORTRAITS OF SOME PIONEERS AND PROMINENT RESIDENTS. NEW YORK: W. W. MUNSELL & COMPANY, 1880. REPRINT, OVID, NEW YORK: W.E. MORRISON & COMPANY, 1976.

JACOBS, DAVID. L. "DOMESTIC SNAPSHOTS: TOWARD A GRAMMAR OF MOTIVES." *JOURNAL OF AMERICAN CULTURE* (4 SPRING 1981), 93-105.

MADDOX, JERALD. "PHOTOGRAPHY AS FOLK ART." IN VAN DEREN COKE, ED. *100 YEARS OF PHOTOGRAPHIC HISTORY: ESSAYS IN HONOR OF BEAUMONT NEWHALL.* ALBUQUERQUE: UNIVERSITY OF NEW MEXICO PRESS, 1975, 104-106.

MANN, MAY BAKER. "PHOTOGRAPHING CHILDREN." *CAMERA CRAFT* (NOVEMBER 1910): 385-390. IN PETER PALMQUIST, *SHADOWCATCHERS: A DIRECTORY OF WOMEN IN CALIFORNIA PHOTOGRAPHY 1900-1920.* ARCATA, CALIFORNIA: 1990.

MOELLER, MADELYN. *NINETEENTH CENTURY WOMEN PHOTOGRAPHERS: A NEW DIMENSION IN LEISURE.* NORWALK, CONNECTICUT: THE LOCKWOOD-MATHEWS MANSION MUSEUM, 1987, 3-4.

MORGAN AND MORGAN, INC. *E. & H. T. ANTHONY & COMPANY ILLUSTRATED CATALOGUE OF PHOTOGRAPHIC EQUIPMENTS AND MATERIALS FOR AMATEURS.* NEW YORK: JOHN POLEMUS, JANUARY, 1891.

MOTZ, MARILYN FERRIS. "VISUAL AUTOBIOGRAPHY: PHOTOGRAPH ALBUMS OF TURN-OF-THE-CENTURY MIDWESTERN WOMEN." *AMERICAN QUARTERLY* 41 (MARCH, 1989): 63-92.

MURRAY, DAVID. *CENTENNIAL HISTORY OF DELAWARE COUNTY, 1797-1897.* DELHI, NEW YORK ; WILLIAM CLARK PUBLISHING COMPANY, 1898.

NEWHALL, BEAUMONT. *THE HISTORY OF PHOTOGRAPHY.* NEW YORK: THE MUSEUM OF MODERN ART, 1982.

ONE HUNDRED AND FIFTY YEARS OF HISTORY FOR THE UNITED METHODIST CHURCH, TREADWELL, NEW YORK. PRIVATELY PRINTED, 1973.

OSTERUD, NANCY GREY. *BONDS OF COMMUNITY: THE LIVES OF FARM WOMEN IN NINETEENTH CENTURY NEW YORK.* ITHACA: CORNELL UNIVERSITY PRESS, 1991.

PALMQUIST, PETER E., ED. *CAMERA FIENDS & KODAK GIRLS: 50 SELECTIONS BY AND ABOUT WOMEN IN PHOTOGRAPHY, 1840 - 1930.* NEW YORK: MIDMARCH ARTS PRESS, 1989.

PALMQUIST, PETER E. *SHADOWCATCHERS: A DIRECTORY OF WOMEN IN CALIFORNIA PHOTOGRAPHY 1900-

1920. Arcata, California: 1990.

Ricca, Barbara Lynn. "The Camera, Bikes and Bloomers." *History of Photography Monograph Number 7*. Privately printed, 1983.

Rockwell, Rev. Charles. *The Catskill Mountains and the Region Around*. Privately printed, 1867; reprint Cornwallville, New York: Hope Farm Press. 1973.

Rosenburg, Rosalind. *Divided Lives: American Women in the Twentieth Century*. New York: The Noonday Press, 1992.

Rothman, Sheila. *Woman's Proper Place: A History of Changing Ideals and Practices, 1870 to the Present*. New York: Basic Books, Inc., 1978.

Schlereth, Thomas J. "Mirrors of the Past: Historical Photography and American History." In Schelereth, ed. *Artifacts and the American Past*. Nashville, Tennessee: American Association for State and Local History, 1980.

Spaulding, H.G. *Spaulding's Business Directory of Delaware County for 1896*. Oneonta, New York: 1896.

Sullivan, Constance. *Women Photographers*. New York: Harry N. Abrahms, Inc., 1990.

Tapley, Daniel J. *The New Recreation: Amateur Photography*. New York: Hurst & Co, 1884.

Trachtenburg, Alan. *Reading American Photographs*. New York: Hill and Wang, 1989.

Tucker, Anne. *The Woman's Eye*. New York: Alfred A. Knopf, 1975.

Wade, Elizabeth Flint. "Amateur Photography Through Women's Eyes, No. 2." *The Photo-American*. 5 (June1894): 235-236.

Watson, Viola H. "The Joy of a Camera." In Peter Palmquist, *Shadowcatchers: A Directory of Women in California Photography 1900-1920*. Arcata, California: 1990.

Williams, Val. *Women Photographers: The Other Observers 1900 to the Present*. London: Virago Press, 1986.

Wilson, E.L. "Velox for the Professional." *Wilson's Photographic Magazine* 37 (September 1900): 411-416. Also in William Welling, *Photography in America: The Formative Years, 1839 - 1900*. New York: Thomas Y. Crowell Company, 1978.

"Woman's [sic] Work in Photography." *The Photographic Times and Amateur Photographer*. 17 (March 18, 1887): 127-128.

Correspondence

Bennett, Mrs. Joseph, Roscoe, New York, to Mrs. George Underwood, Roxbury, New York, 2 April.

Clark, Florence, New York, New York, to Mrs. Underwood, Roxbury, New York, 12 December 1937.

Defender Photo Supply Company, Rochester, New York, to Anna Carroll, Hobart, New York, 28 January 1904.

Dye, Eleanor Carroll, Orchard Park, New York, to Karen Marshall, Cooperstown, New York, 2 March 1992.

Fawcett, Mrs. F.[Nettie], Johnson City, New York, to Lena Underwood, Roxbury, New York, 28 July, and 27 November, 1941.

Miller, Dr. John Adams, Roscoe, New York, to Mrs. George Underwood, Roxbury, New York, 5 December 1938, 11 December 1939 and 18 December 1939.

Snow, Miss Helen G., Yonkers, New York, to Mrs. Underwood, Roxbury, New York, 15 December 1937 and 7 December 1939.

Suter, Patty, Sherborn, Massachusetts, to Lena Underwood, Roxbury, New York, 4 November 1936.

Suttle, Elizabeth, Arena, New York to Mrs. Underwood, Roxbury, New York, 7 January 1942.

Underwood, Ken, Remsenburg, New York, to Karen Marshall, Cooperstown, New York, 6 March 1992.

Interviews

Interviews were conducted by several researchers including Karen Marshall, Diane Galusha and Barbara Davidson with the following individuals:

Benedict, Harry
Benedict, Homer
Blackamer, Christina Georgia Jones
Davidson, Ruth
Dye, Eleanor Carroll
Jackson, John
Kaltenbach, Eleanor
Lyon, Frank and Marjorie
Pogue, Fanny
Rich, Wallace and Helen Rich
Underwood, Dan
Underwood, Ken
White, Florence

Manuscripts

Du Mond, Hanford. "History of the Village of Treadwell from 1896 to February 28, 1922." Treadwell, New York.

Georgia, Stewart Wendell. "Memories of Edna Georgia Benedict, December 1989." [photocopy]. Library, Delaware County Historical Association, Delhi, New York.

Furlow, Elizabeth. "Is Photography Folk Art?" Unpublished paper, Cooperstown, New York: Cooperstown Graduate Program, 1986. New York State Historical Association Special Collections Division.

Jones, Christina Georgia Blackamer. "Memories of Aunt Edna, August 1989." [photocopy]. Library, Delaware County Historical Association, Delhi, New York.

Mead, Eliza, Diary Typescript, 1855-1870, Delaware County Historical Association Library, Delhi, NY.

NICHOLS, ALEXANDER, DIARIES, 1867-1954, DELAWARE COUNTY HISTORICAL ASSOCIATION LIBRARY, DELHI, NY.

PRIME, HELEN OLIVER. "WEST MEREDITH." [PHOTOCOPY]. LIBRARY, DELAWARE COUNTY HISTORICAL ASSOCIATION, DELHI, NEW YORK.

PRIME, HELEN OLIVER. "UNTITLED FEBRUARY 25, 1922." POEM IN THE COLLECTION OF THE TREADWELL UNITED METHODIST CHURCH ARCHIVES, TREADWELL, NEW YORK.

MISCELLANEOUS DOCUMENTS

BENEDICT, HOWARD WESLEY AND EDNA MARY. "STATE OF NEW YORK AFFIDAVIT FOR LICENSE TO MARRY." *NEW YORK STATE DEPARTMENT OF HEALTH BUREAU OF VITAL STATISTICS CERTIFICATE OF RECORD AND MARRIAGE.* DELAWARE COUNTY, TOWN OF MEREDITH. MARRIAGE LICENSE BOOK NO. 4, PAGE 306.

GEORGE MURPHY INC. "CHRISTMAS MASK. A COMPLETE NEW CARD PRODUCTION OUTFIT." MAILED ADVERTISEMENT TO LENA UNDERWOOD.

GRIFFIN, IRMA MAE. *MISCELLANEOUS SCRAPBOOKS, 1930-1932.* TOWN OF ROXBURY VILLAGE LIBRARY, ROXBURY, NEW YORK.

1905 NEW YORK STATE CENSUS, TOWN OF STAMFORD, VILLAGE OF HOBART, DELAWARE COUNTY, FIRST ELECTION DISTRICT, 9.

1927 ROXBURY MARRIAGE LICENSES, NO. 17-252.

TREADWELL UNITED METHODIST CHURCH SUNDAY SCHOOL MINUTES OF MEETINGS, 1941-1947.

NEWSPAPER CLIPPINGS AND NEWSPAPERS

BENEDICT, EDNA. OBITUARY, 3 APRIL 1963. *ONEONTA STAR.* LIBRARY, DELAWARE COUNTY HISTORICAL ASSOCIATION.

CARROLL, ANNA. OBITUARY, 9 AUGUST 1925. *HOBART TIMES.* FROM THE COLLECTION OF FANNY POGUE.

DELAWARE DAIRYMAN, FRANKLIN, NY, SELECTED ISSUES, 1900-1920, FRANKLIN FREE LIBRARY.

DAVIDSON, HOWARD FLETCHER. "A HISTORY OF DELAWARE COUNTY." *COUNTY CONVERSATIONALIST.* 5(3) ALBANY, NEW YORK: COUNTY OFFICERS ASSOCIATION, FEBRUARY 1975.

ROXBURY TIMES, ROXBURY, NY, SELECTED ISSUES, 1890-1940, ROXBURY LIBRARY.

THORINGTON, CHARLES. "CHARLIE'S CORNER." *THE DAILY STAR.* SEPTEMBER 1985. FROM THE COLLECTION OF JOHN JACKSON.

TREADWELL CORRESPONDENT. UNTITLED. RETYPED CLIPPING FROM THE *DELAWARE EXPRESS,* NOVEMBER 29, 1901.

DELAWARE COUNTY HISTORICAL ASSOCIATION

THE DELAWARE COUNTY HISTORICAL ASSOCIATION (DCHA) IS A PRIVATE, NON-PROFIT ORGANIZATION DEDICATED TO COLLECTING, PRESERVING AND INTERPRETING THE HISTORY AND TRADITIONS OF DELAWARE COUNTY, NEW YORK AND THE SURROUNDING CATSKILLS REGION. OUR MISSION IS ACCOMPLISHED THROUGH THE OPERATION OF HISTORIC BUILDINGS, THE COLLECTION AND PRESERVATION OF PAPERS AND ARTIFACTS, RESEARCH, PROGRAMS FOR ALL TYPES OF AUDIENCES, EXHIBITS AND PUBLICATIONS SUCH AS THIS ONE.

FOR MORE INFORMATION ON DCHA'S ACTIVITIES CONTACT:

DCHA

RD #2 BOX 201C

DELHI, NY 13753

607-746-3849